Judy -

To Your Victory!

Duke

Romans 1:16-20

Author's Signed Copies Make Meaningful Gifts!

Order online at www.DUKEDUVALL.com
or phone Toll Free 866-568-9669
HEAR DUKE'S DAILY MESSAGE AT 800-939-LOTW (5689)

"When we shared the platform in a 'tag-team' keynote speech to 2,500 business owners, Duke DuVall impressed me with his unique ability to communicate profound, life-changing principles in a clear and understandable way. In *How to Conquer Giants*, Duke has taken a subject near to my heart—leading our teammates to victory when the sideline critics say it can never be done—and inspires us to lead by example not only on the field, but in every area of life. It's a winner!"

FRAN TARKENTON
NFL HALL OF FAME QUARTERBACK AND AUTHOR OF
WHAT LOSING TAUGHT ME ABOUT WINNING

"In this book is a game plan for victory in life. *How to Conquer Giants* reveals issues we all must face and offers warnings that can prevent big mistakes. DuVall's look at one of the great biblical characters will prove invaluable to anyone who applies the lessons presented."

RAYMOND BERRY
NFL HALL OF FAME RECEIVER AND FORMER HEAD COACH OF
THE NEW ENGLAND PATRIOTS

"How to Conquer Giants is a book that all of us in leadership need to read, comprehend, and put into practice. The book is easy and fun to read, but the important thing is practicing the concepts it contains in the marketplace."

JACK AND GARY KINDER
AUTHORS OF *UPWARD BOUND* AND *21ST CENTURY POSITIONING*

"DuVall uses a very imaginative approach to inspire readers to use their God-given talents and strengths to improve and direct their own lives—and the lives of people around them. Entertaining, valuable."

BENJAMIN S. CARSON SR., M.D.
DIRECTOR OF PEDIATRIC NEUROSURGERY,
JOHNS HOPKINS MEDICINE
PROFESSOR OF NEUROLOGICAL SURGERY, ONCOLOGY,
PLASTIC SURGERY, AND PEDIATRICS, AUTHOR OF *GIFTED HANDS*

"*How to Conquer Giants* is a tremendously inspiring story that proves Old Testament wisdom and principles are more applicable today than ever. It's a book that needs to be read and shared."

CHARLES "T" JONES

AUTHOR OF *LIFE IS TREMENDOUS* AND PRESIDENT OF

EXECUTIVEBOOKS.COM

"The principles and real-life applications within *How to Conquer Giants* are perfect for today's educators. All teachers, students, and parents could benefit from applying these lessons to their individual situations."

DR. DEBRA PEPPERS

NATIONAL TEACHERS HALL OF FAME

"This book prepares the reader for the battlefields of life and the enemies of our souls. Identifying and annihilating one's personal giants is essential to any warrior who's heaven-bent on impacting his world and leaving a legacy for others to follow."

"Success and inheritance are often measured in financial terms. Duke DuVall challenges our traditional preconceptions and raises the bar to establish a legacy which neither moth nor rust can corrupt."

ED BISSONNETTE

FOCUS ON THE FAMILY

HOW TO

CONQUER

GIANTS

THE TOP TEN SUCCESS PRINCIPLES FROM THE WORLD'S RICHEST MAN

Duke DuVall

Multnomah®Publishers *Sisters, Oregon*

HOW TO CONQUER GIANTS
published by Multnomah Publishers, Inc.

© 2001 by Duke DuVall

International Standard Book Number: 1-57673-784-5

Cover design by Chris Gilbert/Uttley DouPonce Design Works
Cover art/photo by Tony Stone Images

Scripture quotations are from:
The Holy Bible, New International Version © 1973, 1984 by
International Bible Society, used by permission of
Zondervan Publishing House

Multnomah is a trademark of Multnomah Publishers, Inc.,
and is registered in the U.S. Patent and Trademark Office.
The colophon is a trademark of Multnomah Publishers, Inc.

Printed in the United States of America

For information:
MULTNOMAH PUBLISHERS, INC.
POST OFFICE BOX 1720
SISTERS, OREGON 97759

Library of Congress Cataloging–in–Publication Data
DuVall, Duke.
How to conquer giants : the top ten success principles from the
world's richest man / by Duke DuVall.   p.cm.
ISBN 1-57673-784-5
1. Success–Religious aspects–Christianity. I. Title.
BV4598.3 .D88 2001   248.4–dc21   00-013197

01 02 03 04 05—10 9 8 7 6 5 4 3 2 1 0

TABLE OF CONTENTS

INTRODUCTION

How big would you make your goals if you knew you couldn't fail? How would your life be different if you had your very own success coach to help you make any dream come true and to see that you conquered every obstacle in your path? And what if your personal advisor just happened to be the wealthiest and wisest man in the world?

Enter the great king of Israel. The construction of his personal residence, along with the temple, required 80,000 stonecutters and a building crew of 3,600 foremen overseeing an additional 70,000 workers. The palace staff numbers 5,000 attendants, who meet the needs of the great king, his children, and his 700 wives. All of his table settings are made of pure gold. His personal income exceeds $10 million per week, and a prized collection of 12,000 Arabian horses is divided among the royal family's numerous country estates. But his wisdom is even greater than his wealth.

Prior to his ascension to the throne, his nation was embroiled in wars for over four decades. Under his foreign policy, Israel has now enjoyed forty years of uninterrupted peace. His domestic policy for economic development has made "silver as commonplace as stones" throughout his kingdom. With captivating brilliance he instructs vast armies on military strategies; advises foreign heads of state on matters of public policy; forecasts economic conditions years into the future.

So what goals would you attempt if you knew you couldn't fail? If no giant, obstacle, or challenge stood in your way? Well, dream big. After reading *How to Conquer Giants: The Top Ten Success Principles from the World's Richest Man,* you'll have a whole new appreciation for what it means to be "more than a conqueror"!

CHAPTER ONE

THE KING OF THE GIANT CONQUERORS

As a boy, I loved hearing the stories of the adventures of my father, the great King David. I loved hearing about his military exploits, about how he bravely fought and won battles on behalf of my God and my people, the Israelites.

Later, when I became a man, when I was no longer referred to as King David's son but as King Solomon, I still loved hearing the stories about how my father led his people to victory after victory over their enemies, over those who wanted more than anything to end the nation of Israel's existence.

By then, my father's military and political reputation had become legendary throughout Israel. People from all segments of our population—from children to those who had fought at my father's side in the army of Israel—knew about the things King David had done on our behalf.

While the accounts of my father's exploits are too numerous to list here, there was one story that most everyone agrees stands out as central to my father's legacy as a great fighting man and leader of our people. It is the story of his victorious battle with the Philistine giant named Goliath.

If my father ever grew weary of my begging him to relive the vivid details of the battle for my friends and me, he never let on. I know I never grew weary of hearing it, even after I had become a man. And I've never grown weary of telling the story of the brave young man who saved our entire nation from certain defeat at the hands of the mighty Philistine army.

Later on I'll give you more details of the battle, but right now I'd like to start our time together by relaying to you the incidents, as they have been told to me so many times, that led to my father's life-and-death confrontation with the mighty warrior of the Philistine army.

S tanding before the army of the nation of Israel was what could only be seen as a threat to its very existence. The Philistine army, its goal to take from Israel what God had given her, had gathered for war against God's people, and leading this great army was an awesome fighting man by the name of Goliath.

This giant, standing more than nine feet tall and weighing over 450 pounds, was an awesome soldier. He knew that no one could stand up to him man-to-man. He was massive and powerful, but he was also an elite fighting machine. Not a single soldier in Israel's army wanted to square off with the dreaded killer.

For nearly six weeks, day after day, night after night, the

two armies faced each other down as Goliath threatened the Israelites and even cursed their God as he challenged any-one—just *one* man—to come forward and fight. When forty days had passed and not one member of Israel's army had volunteered to stand against the giant, a shepherd boy named David stepped forward and told King Saul that he would do battle with the Philistine.

At first King Saul couldn't believe that David was ready to go to war with Goliath. "You are only a boy, and he has been a fighting man since his youth," Saul told him.[1] But the brave teenager persisted in pleading his case with the king. "I killed a lion and a bear when they attacked my sheep," David told Saul. "God was with me then, and He'll be with me when I fight the Philistine."[2] Reluctantly, Saul agreed to allow the shepherd boy to do battle with this seemingly insurmountable foe. But I emphasize *seemingly* insurmount-able. If I've learned anything from my father's courageous stand it's that what truly matters is not the size of the man in the fight but rather the size of the fight in the man.

He had warded off every predator from his father Jesse's flock. Now it was David's chance, as he saw it, to protect his heavenly Father's flock. It was no longer the safety of just a few dozen lambs that hung in the balance. It was the future of an entire nation's freedom that rested in the hands—skill-ful though they were—of a boy who "just happened to be" delivering food to his soldier brothers.

Down in the flatland of the Valley of Elah, the only natural barrier separating the shepherd boy from the terrifying giant was a meager brook. Its bed was shallow enough and its water clear enough that David could have seen every rock on the bottom. But he didn't. Even as he hurriedly helped himself to five choice stones, David's eyes never left Goliath. From the moment he emerged from his commander's tent and began his descent down the mountain toward the battle line, his focus never deviated. Young David already knew one of the fundamental secrets to conquering giants: Once you commit to conquering a giant, do not let anything distract your attention until the job is done.

From the beginning, our future king was a natural when it came to bringing down giants. Years of practice protecting his father's flock from wild animals had prepared the shepherd boy's hands for selecting just the right stones without actually looking at them. At the brook he hoped to fully replenish his supply. The animal-hide pouch could easily accommodate a dozen or more round stones, ever ready to be hurled at lions and bears and, if necessary, nine-foot-plus giants.

When I think about this pivotal moment in the history of my people, I can close my eyes and almost hear my father tell me, "Solomon, remember that it's always better to have resources and not need them than to need them and not have them. So pray as if everything depends on God's power and then prepare as though everything depends on your preparations. Then proceed with the task at hand. Pray. Prepare. Proceed."

That day David did just that. He prayed up, stocked up, and showed up. All of this just in time—without a moment to spare. At nearly ten feet tall and weighing more than 450 pounds, the giant closed fast. Despite the fact that he was wearing more than two hundred pounds of armor and weapons, this human tank possessed amazing agility and speed. Goliath's shield bearer, who was close to David's age and size, was at an all-out run to keep up with the huge strides the Philistine warrior made as he charged the battle line.

David plunged both hands into the shallow brook. Working totally by touch, the boy's ten fingers searched the bottom quickly, yet carefully, to select just the right stones. With thousands of eyes riveted on him and time quickly running out, he had to remain calm and make each selection with precision. It was his last chance to add to what already seemed, to both armies, too little too late.

Nevertheless, this meager stockpile of weapons—the five smooth, spherical stones he had chosen—now sat ready in his shepherd's pouch. The first-time warrior stood to his full height of five feet and quickly dried his hands by shaking them and rubbing his palms against his legs. His gaze, right into the giant's eyes, never wavered.

David could have thought about the dozen stones he had wanted to gather. He could have lamented the fact that he had only had time to grab five. But in the heat of any battle it's always counterproductive to dwell on what you don't have. Instead, David chose to focus on what he *did* have—five smooth stones, each one carefully, prayerfully selected. He vaulted from the brook and ran to the battle line. The slope of the opposing mountains served as a grandstand for the spectators who were riveted to this showdown. As two of the most powerful armies in the world watched in amazement, every Philistine and Israelite soldier facing off at Elah that day could agree on at least one thing: In the next few minutes, one of these brave warriors would be dead.

CHAPTER TWO

So You Want to Conquer Giants

I started this book by describing the events leading up to my father's very first battle with Goliath in order to present this message against a backdrop of what I believe is a classic illustration of good triumphing over evil against seemingly insurmountable odds—at least by human standards.

If, by some remote chance, you have never heard the story of the battle between David and Goliath, the fact that I am here to bring you this message should tell you the ultimate outcome of that fight. As I proceed with my message, I will give you more details of this now-classic confrontation. I will tell you about how the man who would later be king of my people overcame the odds to become a hero in the eyes of Israel and in the hearts of much of the rest of the world.

For now, however, I want to shift our discussion from the details of David's battle with Goliath to our own battles with the giants—I would refer to those as "personal giants"—who want to thwart us in our quest for true and lasting success.

When I talk about these "personal giants," I am not referring to literal physical giants like the one my father faced all those years ago. These are not flesh-and-blood giants who come against us with swords, spears, and javelins. They aren't even necessarily giants who want to end our physical existence, although that can be a part of the equation. Rather, these are inner giants who come against us using our human attributes—our so-called strengths as well as our weaknesses—to defeat us and rob us.

There is no topic I love teaching more than that of conquering personal giants. When I think of battling and defeating giants, my soul is stirred to its very core. Perhaps that is partially because of the obvious sentimental value this topic, in its most literal sense, holds within my own family and within the culture of my people.

I myself have drawn great encouragement and inspiration from the story of my father's victory over the Philistine Goliath, and I believe you can, too. I believe any of us can look at how the shepherd boy with no experience in warfare felled a great warrior giant who threatened his people.

I also love this particular topic because it is, in a very real way, a collaborated effort between my father and me. My father was a wonderful musician and lyricist, and he taught me an appreciation for music. We collaborated on many songs over the years, and if the topic of defeating giants were a song, then my father would have partially written its lyrics, then passed them on to me during the time he was king of Israel and I was his student. I would have written the remainder of this "song" based on what I have learned during my reign as king about conquering my own giants.

More than all of this, however, I love this topic because I know that each and every one of us, during some point in our lives, will have to do battle with at least one of the giants I'm going to discuss. Whether or not we enjoy genuine, lasting success in life will hinge on the outcome of our battles.

I love to see people defeat their personal giants, then go on to enjoy truly successful lives, lives that leave rich legacies for their children and their children's children. My family is a living example that this approach indeed works.

My father defeated the literal giant Goliath, then he defeated several other deadly personal giants as well. And because he won the victories over these giants, he was great—as a man of God, as a loving husband and father, and as a valiant leader.

I will be candid with you today and tell you that my family and I have been enormously blessed in this lifetime. My father, despite his own personal moral failings (I will discuss that later), was an overwhelming success as a military leader and as king of Israel. For forty years he brilliantly and faithfully led his people in victorious battle against all their enemies, both foreign and domestic.

My father left for me—and for *my* children, for that matter—a tremendous legacy on many fronts. He left for me a mighty kingdom, and that has led to an accumulation of incredible material wealth for me, my family, and my associates. I have been described as the world's wealthiest man.

Indeed, my kingdom has been blessed with wealth that is greater than many of the world's kingdoms combined. In addition to that, I have been blessed with tremendous power, as well as the respect of fellow leaders around the world.

More important than all the material wealth and power my father left me, however, is his legacy of wisdom. He taught me much about what it means to be a true success, the kind of success that leaves a legacy that lasts long after one passes on from this life. Having received such a blessing through my father, I now believe that it is my duty to ensure that the seeds of wisdom he planted in me—which I readily and joyfully acknowledge have resulted in whatever good that can be seen in me—bear fruit in the lives of others, both now and in future generations.

As this lesson progresses, we'll discuss my list of the top ten giants people face on their way to what I call the promised land of ultimate success. You may face just a few of these giants, or you may face *all* of them at some point in your life. But make no mistake, you *will* eventually have to face one or more of these giants.

My goal today is to give you the motivation and the know-how in battling and defeating the personal giants whose only reason for existence is to keep you from grabbing hold of complete and lasting success.

But before I do that I'd like to start by defining the nature of the personal giants we face and some basics for battling and defeating them effectively. In addition, I'd like to talk about our reason for going to war against these giants.

I n this fallen world in which we live, personal giants are a fact of life. I can guarantee you that you will be confronted by one of the ten giants I'm going to identify later on. Perhaps at this very moment you are in the same position my father was in all those years ago: facing the prospect of a battle with a giant who wants more than anything to destroy you.

When you stand face-to-face with one of these personal giants, you have only two options: conquer the giant with finality or surrender and accept defeat. Believe me, you won't be able to negotiate a peaceful coexistence with one of these personal giants any more than the Israelites could have peacefully negotiated with Goliath, who wanted to humiliate them, steal their land, and take them into captivity.

These are dangerous giants, giants who prefer a "take no prisoners" approach. They are well armed, experienced warriors who show no mercy when they have us in their sights. In that respect they are much like the Philistine soldier my father faced on the battlefield so many years ago.

We have no way of knowing exactly how many lives the giant Goliath destroyed before young David brought his reign of terror to an end. Likewise, there is no way of knowing how many more lives he would have taken had David not destroyed him. I know that from a purely military standpoint Goliath was a fierce warrior. He was majestic and powerful in his two hundred pounds of glistening battle armor, and he was armed with a bronze javelin and a spear with an iron point that weighed fifteen pounds alone.

Goliath was deadly not just because he was a huge man

who was well armed. He was a great warrior because he had what we might refer to as a "killer instinct," that dark part of him that actually enjoyed slaughtering his enemies. He was in no way merciful toward those who stood in his way; rather, he was a ruthless killing machine. And he was cunning in the ways of war, having fought and won countless battles on behalf of his people. There was even talk that when the Philistines weren't at war, Goliath hired himself as a mercenary to other armies, so great was his lust for killing.

This impressive, frightening soldier, the one the official record describes as "a champion,"[1] gave the Israelites but one choice: "Defeat me or be defeated. Kill me or die yourself."[2] There would be no negotiations with Goliath and his people, only a battle that ended in someone's death. And when this man-to-man death match was over, one of these mighty armies was going to be routed and their property taken.

That is how personal giants operate. Their focus is on your destruction, on taking what is yours. And once they have laid down a challenge, they will never back down or negotiate some kind of peaceful agreement. To them there is only one way to win a battle, and that is with a fight to the very finish.

As perverse as it may seem to most of us, a giant would rather die in battle than negotiate at the table of reason. That is why we must be ruthless and merciless when we deal with our personal giants. We can't simply capture, coddle, or correct giants. We must defeat them with extreme aggression. Even when they beg us for mercy, we must finish what we started when we engage them in battle.

Like it or not, our personal giants' refusal to compromise

or back off in the face of negotiations defines the scope of the alternatives for those of us who wish to attain lasting success. We must either battle and conquer our giants with finality or be defeated on the battlefield.

You can't negotiate with these giants, nor can you avoid them forever. I can guarantee that sooner or later, one or more of these giants will assault you. He will stubbornly continue to call you out to battle, much the way Goliath called out for just one member of the army of Israel to come out and fight him to the finish.[3]

The giants we will be discussing later are, for a fact, vicious warriors. They are relentless and merciless in their attacks. But know this: They can be conquered! We can be victorious in our battles with them. With the proper preparation and strategic forethought we can determine where and how the battle will take place. And we can conquer the giants who challenge us to fight.

I f we want to achieve true and lasting success in this life, then we must know a little something about battling and defeating our personal giants. We need to know what kinds of giants these are that come against us and what kinds of tactics they use. We need to know which of our weaknesses they like to attack as well as how to neutralize their strengths using the right weapons against them.

Simply wishing for true and lasting success doesn't work; neither will just moving in whatever direction our whims take us. We need to have a vision of our goals when we approach our quest for lasting success. We need to know what it is we are trying to attain in this life, then take the appropriate steps to attain it. In light of that, if we are to reach the promised land of lasting success, we will have to defeat the giants who stand in our way and bellow challenges at us. Before we can understand *how* to conquer giants, we have to grasp the all-important *why*.

I have a friend who is a very successful merchant, and he underscores the "why before the how" learning principle when he says, "A man who knows *how* will always have a job, but he'll always be working for the man who knows *why*." In other words, know-how is a valuable asset, but it will always take a backseat to knowing *why* we are even interested in the know-how to begin with.

How speaks to the heart of the method, but *why* speaks to the heart of the man. *How* defines the techniques we use to destroy giants. *Why* defines the vision, reflects the motivation, and reminds us of the mission. This is crucial because without vision we will perish at the hands of our giants.[4]

Friends, before you go into battle with a giant, it is absolutely essential that you define your motivation for fighting. You need a vision of what the giant is preventing you from achieving. Knowing what it takes to defeat a giant and having the passion to defeat him are great, but you need to know your reason for fighting in the first place.

You see, giants love to do battle with people who lack vision, people who aren't sure of their motivation. My father, whose vision never wavered when he stood against Goliath, never tired of warning me, "When you are face-to-face with a giant bent on destroying you, your vision will determine your passion. And your passion will strongly predict whether you are the conqueror or the conquered."

My people, the Israelites, are familiar with one point in our history when the vision of two brave, focused men helped lead to our taking the original Promised Land. Our forefather Moses dispatched a leader from each of the twelve tribes of Israel to explore the land of Canaan. Moses left little to chance when he sent the spies. He instructed the twelve to explore the land itself. They were to see if the soil in the land was fruitful and good. They were to see what crops the land produced. They were also to take a look at the cities that had been erected there and see if they were fortified for war. And they were to look at the enemy and see if they were strong or weak.

After forty days of scouting Canaan, all twelve of these leaders agreed on one thing: It was, indeed, the beautiful, fruitful land God had promised them. But ten of these men—those who had no vision for claiming what had been divisively granted to them—came back terrified and unified in their negative report. "We can never possess this land," they protested. "There are giants in the land! We can never attack them and expect to win. If we battle these people, we will die!"

The other two scouts—Joshua and Caleb, who kept their eyes on the ultimate mission—also came back with a unified report. But it was a positive one because their vision was clear and their faith was strong. "The land we passed through and explored is exceedingly good," they reported. "Are there some challenges? Sure. Never mind the giants! We *can* possess our land! We *must* possess our land!"[5]

Centuries later David, the young shepherd boy who kept

his focus on the goal before him and who was filled with the same kind of faith as Joshua and Caleb, gave a similar reply when Goliath threatened his people: "Don't anyone worry about this giant. I'll go out and fight him!"6

With that, the stage was set for the classic showdown between good and evil. The boy who would later be my father, and who would later rule as king of Israel, was about to face off with the giant Goliath. At that key moment, the shepherd David's future, and the very future of the nation of Israel, was at stake.

It was at that moment that my father, through an act of obedience and astounding courage, motivated by a prophetic vision of the calling in life God had planned for him, established for himself a legacy of greatness.

You might say that "created for greatness" was a theme in my father's life from the very beginning. Through a sovereign calling, David was set apart and prepared for greatness from the time he was a boy.7 Before my father had even heard of the Philistine warrior Goliath, the events in his life pointed him toward this dramatic, historic showdown and toward continued greatness as the leader of God's chosen people, the Israelites.

If I close my eyes I can almost hear my father's voice: "Solomon, even after I became king, some of my critics called me 'David the shepherd boy.' But critics don't count. God spoke to me when I really was a shepherd and what matters is that even then He called me 'David the king.'" In this respect, my father's life should serve as a reminder to all of us that everything up to a given point in our lives is but a rehearsal for what lies ahead. And while those with no vision whine, "I'll believe it when I see it," people of faith proclaim, "You'll see it when you believe it!"

Created for greatness! It was the truth in my father's life and in my life as well. The same is true for you. Each and every one of us has been created for some sort of greatness. Not all of us are created to lead our nations to glorious victory over our enemies. Not all of us are called to serve as king of our people. Not all of us are called to be wealthy in the material sense. But we are all called to greatness in some arena of this life.

I believe that we are made to have a vision, made to dream. And our visions and dreams for our lives are not to achieve mediocrity. Rather, we are made to do great things on behalf of our families, our nations, and our God. And one of the most agreed-upon measures of greatness is not what you attain, but rather the magnitude of the obstacles you overcome to attain it.

No legend springs forth when a shepherd boy removes a fly or a tick from a lamb, for there is no sacrifice, no risk of loss in conquering them. It is a shepherd's duty to protect and care for his sheep. Because of that, no one would consider it an extraordinary achievement even when that shepherd rescues some of his lambs from a wild animal such as a lion or a bear. The shepherd is, after all, charged with protecting his sheep from those kinds of threats, too. But though these ordinary acts don't make the shepherd great, they do make him faithful. And once we are faithful in little, we can be made rulers over much.[8]

If we want to be truly great, if we want to reach the promised land of ultimate success, then we will need to be faithful in the ordinary to prepare us for the extraordinary. You'll never be successful in overcoming the giant-sized obstacles until you're faithful in defeating the lion-sized obstacles. But you're not ever going to be prepared for victory over lions until you've proven your faithfulness in the mundane and routine task of eliminating those pesky flies. Like David, you will have to battle and defeat the personal giants whose only goal, whose only reason for existence, is to disarm you and destroy you. And like David, it will be your faithfulness in the ordinary that prepares you for the extraordinary.

But be on guard. Because even when you've graduated from flies to lions and are now ready to conquer giants, not all giants you face will look like Goliath. Believe me, conquering them would be much easier if they did. The giants we face will come in many different forms, some of which will seem innocent, or even beneficial, to us. That is why I am passing along to you the things I've learned from my father and from personal experience about winning the war against giants.

It is my hope that as you walk with me through this lesson you will learn to recognize giants when you see them, then to do the things it takes to defeat them soundly and with finality. When you apply the disciplines it takes to conquer one giant, you are well on your way to conquering other giants, too.

S o, if you're ready, let's get started. As we prepare to
tackle giant number ten in our countdown to the ten
most important giants to be conquered, let me give
you an important warning: Just because number ten isn't a
loud and intimidating giant doesn't mean he isn't just as
deadly as the other nine. I learned that the hard way. This
giant nearly killed me.

CHAPTER THREE

THE SUBTLE GIANT: DISCONTENT

It's hard to imagine such a thing as a subtle giant. Giants are supposed to look and behave like the one my father felled all those years ago. They're supposed to be ferocious, merciless, and overwhelming. They're supposed to have bulging muscles, thick armor, and hard hearts, all of which they use when they declare war on us.

Giants are too big to sneak up on anyone. They rely on brute strength, superior weaponry, and a knowledge of warfare to overwhelm us and take what they want, even our very lives if they so choose. They don't approach us with humility, either. They know they will win—in a rout. They come at us with looks of disdain on their faces, as if we're some kind of annoyance they know they won't need to work up a sweat to defeat.

There was nothing subtle about Goliath the Philistine. He stood over nine feet tall and was adorned head to toe with hundreds of pounds of armor. He mocked his enemy, challenging the Israelites daily to send just one man brave enough to fight him. He had been a warrior since his youth, and he knew there wasn't a single soldier in Israel's army who could stand against him.

Unlike Goliath, merciless killers don't always roar with thunderous threats. A subtle giant does exist. He's big and strong, and he has all the power he needs, if we give it to him, to destroy us. He knows how to kill us slowly, from the inside out, by feeding us one lie after another until we are robbed of our energy, our joy for life, our purpose for existence.

This giant's name is Discontent. He is subtle because he's the overgrown, out-of-control version of what can be a wise, sound approach to life—the approach that tells us that we can be successful, even wealthy, if we work hard and honestly to attain and appropriately handle what we have.

The giant named Discontent mocks us and tells us that we deserve what we don't or cannot have. He makes us believe that somehow life hasn't given us what we have coming to us, that life has treated us unfairly. This giant overtakes us by whispering in our ear that if what we have is good, more would be even better. He focuses our attention on those who have what we want but don't have. He inspires within us every form of jealousy, resentment, and selfish ambition.

Discontent is a subtle giant, but he's every bit as deadly as Goliath. Discontent is at the heart of so many human problems. The insatiable desire for more and better ruins lives, destroys families, stunts businesses, and sends nations to war. In fact, my father had to square off with Goliath because the giant named Discontent had already infected the entire Philistine army. The discontented Philistines wanted to take from the people of Israel the land that had been divinely appointed to us.

The Subtle Giant: Discontent

We have to deal with the giant named Discontent with finality. He is not a giant that can be controlled or put in his place. On the contrary, if we are to live full, rich lives, we must slay this giant once and for all.

O kay, I know what you are thinking: "What would King Solomon, the richest man in the world, know about discontent? He has everything he could ever want or need, so how could he possibly know anything about wanting or needing something he doesn't have?"

In one respect, that is a valid point. But it is also one of the main points this cunning killer uses to trick us into letting down our guard.

I have lived a life of wealth, and I don't have need of anything—at least not in the physical sense. I was blessed with wealth beyond most people's imagination. Never a day went by that I wanted for anything in the material sense. On the other hand, the life I have led, with its extraordinary material abundance, has taught me that no matter how much one possesses, there is still the danger of becoming discontented, of wanting more.

Does it surprise you that even the wealthiest man in the world could, if he weren't careful, be cleverly pulled into a struggle with this giant named Discontent? Don't believe for a moment that envy plagues only those who are still struggling to get by, that greed and jealousy and an obsession with wanting more doesn't ensnare the rich. I tell you—from personal experience, no less—that the heart of a man who lives in a palace and has untold riches at his disposal can become corrupted with ingratitude and discontentment.

I'm not proud of the fact that I spent a great deal of my life obsessed with accomplishing great things, with acquiring and doing more. I did just that, too! I amassed more wealth and possessions than all who went before me in Jerusalem, more than the combined treasuries of several countries.

I have built house after house, planted vineyard after vineyard, garden after garden and orchard after orchard. I have bigger herds and flocks than all who ever lived here before me. I have gathered for myself silver and gold and the special treasures of kings and of all the provinces. All of my drinking vessels—in my palace and in my forest retreat—are made of pure gold.

I have 12,000 horses, 1,400 chariots, and 12,000 horsemen at my disposal. They are stationed this very day in the chariot cities here under the direction of my palace guard. I hired more servants than anyone in the history of the world. I have at my immediate call singers, entertainers, and musical instruments of all kinds.

What I've listed here is just a fraction of the wealth I've accumulated over the years. And though I am wealthier than any of the kings of the world, I've come to one pretty shocking revelation concerning my riches: When I get my focus off of what is truly important, there's never enough!

That's the way it is when you love material riches. No matter how much you have, it's never enough to satisfy. No matter how many horses or chariots I acquire, no matter how much gold I have in the storehouse, no matter how many servants are at my disposal—if I place my love with these riches, my existence will be empty and meaningless.[1]

What I'm talking about here is being possessed by our possessions, being controlled by the things we are called to control. There is nothing wrong with attaining wealth, but when we become servants to that wealth, we have fallen prey to the giant named Discontent. So many have swallowed the lie that yearning for "more" is nothing but a harmless pastime. But I tell you that money will never satisfy, because when you make acquiring money your focus in life, you will always want more. The same is true of chasing power or fame.

My friends, the measure of someone's satisfaction isn't in the size of his bank account or in the vastness of his mansion. That can only be measured by what is inside the person. And if what lies inside that person is discontent, envy, jealousy, selfish ambition, and the love of money, that person's life will be an exercise in futility. It will simply be the vain pursuit of more riches for riches' sake.

You can enjoy the fruits of your labor, and you can make use of the wealth you have earned. But when enjoyment and utilization of these things becomes a love for them, you will never be satisfied.

Enough will never be enough.

My father, King David of Israel, acquired great wisdom during his days on this earth, and I can gratefully tell you that he passed much of that wisdom on to me. One of the great truths he taught me was that we should not tie our contentment to our earthly treasures or circumstances. His attitude was that if God was with him, it didn't matter if he was wealthy or living hand-to-mouth, because he had all that he needed.

It was easy for many who knew my father to forget that he didn't always live as a king but that he started out as a simple shepherd boy. He knew what it was like to live in wealth, but he also knew very well what it was like to live on little. King David lived through some of the "tough times" in Israel's early existence. And through it all, he learned to be grateful for what he had, genuinely believing "that all things work together for good to them that love God, to them that are called to his purpose."[2]

I've enjoyed my success and my riches. But I've learned, through my own experiences and those of my father, that each person's station in life—whether that person is rich, poor, or something in-between—has its own unique tests and trials.

I have heard many people muse about how life would be so much different, so much easier, if they were wealthy. Then, they reason, there would be no stress in their lives over money, because all their needs would be readily met.

I would counter that way of thinking by pointing out that wealth can be a source of tremendous anxiety for the rich person. There's something about making the acquisition of money a central goal in life that brings stress. I like to tell people that the common working man sleeps better at night, no matter how little or how much he has, but that the maintenance of a rich man's wealth can keep him awake at night.[3]

The wealthy man—and I know what I'm talking about here, friends—has worries most other people don't have. He has to worry about whether his latest business venture will be a success or a failure, whether it will bring him even more riches or bankruptcy.

When someone makes the quest for wealth his life's goal, he sets himself up for devastation when the wealth doesn't come or, worse yet, when he gains then loses it.

My father spoke to me on numerous occasions about what happened to Saul, the first king of Israel, when he put his trust in earthly resources. He was let down. My father delivered the king and his army from Goliath once and for all. But he had to deliver Saul from the giant named Discontent on numerous occasions.

That's the price we pay for putting our trust in possessions or positions. When our riches or popularity fail us—and make no mistake, they *will* fail us eventually—we are left having trusted that which is fallible and temporal. When that happens, we are left with nothing but our disillusionment and disappointment.

At that point, the giant named Discontent has defeated us in battle. For the multitudes who never regroup, he has won the entire war.

I t is vanity and pure folly to tie our lasting happiness, contentment, and peace of mind to anything that cannot possibly last. When we do that, we build our lives on what is at best an unstable, untrustworthy foundation. That is because the wealth of even the richest of the rich is temporal and can be gone in an instant.

Though I am the richest man in the history of Israel, I

realize that all I possess can be taken from me in but an instant or that I can be taken from it. Both pauper and king bring nothing into this world at birth and that is exactly how they make their exits. This realization has brought me to the point of making sure I don't place my security in what I own.

There's some part of our fallen humanity that tempts us to place our security and our worth in the acquisition of riches. But is it true security to trust something that can vanish overnight? Is it good to place our self-worth in what can disappear in but a moment?

If we were to measure a person's worth or quality of life by his wealth or prominence, then we could assume that the man who amasses the greatest wealth or is the most politically powerful is the happiest, most respected, and most contented person on the planet. But you and I both know that is utter foolishness. We all know very wealthy and powerful people who are not respected, who are insecure, and who live as slaves to the giant named Discontent.

Truly, there are things that money just cannot buy and that power cannot dictate.

I have learned that true security, true happiness, and true contentment are not the results of temporary riches or fleeting power but are founded upon godly wisdom. I have learned that a life based on such a philosophy is a genuinely happy existence, and that godly wisdom is worth far more than any of my earthly treasures. It is that eternal wisdom, and not my earthly riches, that has made my life long and truly prosperous.[4]

When we come to the point of grasping that truth, we find out what true riches really are.

I don't want anything I've said here today to be taken as a discouragement from working hard and from becoming prosperous, for wealth properly attained is itself a gift and a blessing. Indeed, there is nothing wrong with being wealthy or working to produce wealth. God is not opposed to our having wealth, but rather to wealth having us.

Moses, the great leader of the Israelites, often reminded the people that every good and perfect gift comes from above—even the ability to produce wealth.[5] I encourage you to take part in honest, hard work. In fact, I would warn anyone against being lazy or complacent in this life, for hard work is the only way to properly attain material wealth.

The trap you must avoid, however, is that of being motivated to work out of a selfish desire for more and more. There is nothing wrong with ambition, but you must be careful that your ambition doesn't become the very sword the giant named Discontent uses against you, to pierce your soul!

I also don't want to suggest that there is anything inherently wrong with admiring other people's achievements, gifts, or attributes. It's good to admire what our neighbor has accomplished in life, to respect those who have attained high positions through their honest effort, to appreciate the physical beauty or talents of those around us.

But when that simple admiration turns to envy or resentment—obsessing over what another person has—it becomes another weapon in the hands of the assassin named Discontent.

Almost since the beginning of time, we humans have struggled with this clever enemy—that belligerent giant within who makes us want more and more of what he convinces us will make life better but really causes us to live lives filled with jealousy and envy. Discontent will destroy everything about us if we allow him to.

My father fought a belligerent giant. Day and night, for a month and a half, Goliath came roaring and bellowing curses at the Israelites, yet our soldiers refused to challenge him. The giant grew bolder and more arrogant by the day, knowing no one had the courage to face him on the battlefield.

Goliath was not going to go away, and neither will this giant named Discontent, who inflicts on us greed and envy and covetousness. On the contrary, he will grow more stubborn and belligerent by the day if we don't face up to him and defeat him.

My father, David, just a shepherd boy at the time, stopped the great Philistine warrior cold with one well-placed stone to the forehead. But what is the "stone" that will stop this formidable foe named Discontent?

I believe the weapon of choice is a heart full of gratitude. You need to realize that everything you have—not just your wealth but your ability to produce wealth; not just your position but the influence your prominence affords—is a gift, divinely wrapped and delivered. When you recognize that fact, you can develop in your heart a deep gratitude for all you have and, believe it or not, for what you don't have.

My father had a wonderful sense of humor. He once told me, "Solomon, imagine if Noah and his wife had displayed an attitude similar to that of most people. Rather than being thankful that they had been spared in the great flood, they would have gotten off of the ark and said 'What a lousy cruise—it rained for the first month and a half!'"

That's how the giant named Discontent operates. In his grip, he will make your entire journey through life a miserable trip.

Remember, not so much as one penny of what we possess in this lifetime will follow us past the grave. When we die, it won't matter one bit how much material wealth we possess. We are born with nothing—not even a covering of clothes—and after we die, we will stand before our Maker with nothing.[6]

Work hard to accomplish things in this life, but be content with what you have. You've been given a promise that you will never be forsaken. Embrace the spirit of humble thanksgiving, and you will soundly conquer the first giant on your path to true riches and lasting success. When you have done that, the good news is that you are now an official giant conqueror. The bad news is that you have just made the nine remaining giants very angry.

CHAPTER FOUR

THE BEGUILING GIANT: DECEPTION

He is a powerful and cruel giant. In just an instant he can destroy our friends, our families, our neighbors. He's a giant who can cause devastating harm to us, to those around us, and to the reputation of what we are and whom we represent. He's not a giant who carries weapons of wood or iron. But he is able—if we don't control him—to destroy and kill all the same.

I'm talking about the giant named Deception.

Our words have untold power to bless, but they can do equally untold harm when we don't speak truthfully. Lives can be destroyed with deceptive words. Reputations can be ruined by well-placed lies. Dreams can be dashed when someone is misled for the benefit of another. We can speak truthfully, or we can speak deceitfully. Life and death is in the tongue.[1] Therefore, if we want to achieve true greatness, if we want a life of happiness, contentment, and blessing, we must conquer this giant named Deception. We must be sure we speak truthfully in every way.

Our law included the words, "You shall not bear false testimony against your neighbor."[2] From our youth we were also instructed, "Do not spread false reports."[3]

My father taught me early how important and wise it is to restrain my mouth and to make sure I always speak truthfully, that I don't in any way convey false information or impressions. He continually reminded me of the importance of making sure that neither my words nor my actions contained even a hint of deception.

"Never give false testimony against your neighbor. Don't speak deceitfully. And when you speak of another, make sure you don't speak untruthfully," King David told me. "When you do those things, it not only hurts people and ruins reputations, but it also dishonors all that is holy."

The giant named Deception is a deadly one, and sooner or later we will have to defeat him with finality to enter the promised land of lasting success. As with each of the giants, finishing him offer sooner than later is a good idea.

When I use the word *deception,* I'm referring to the use of our speech to present—through the telling of outright lies, the use of "twisted truth," malicious gossip, or flattery—an inaccurate picture of the facts.

Deception can ruin relationships. It can cause us to take that to which we are not entitled by cheating others—a sure path to destruction. Deception clutters our minds and hardens our hearts as we scramble to remember our latest fabrication so as to "keep our story straight."

Deception has been at the center of many human problems since the beginning of history. In my culture we are taught the story of Adam and Eve, who were placed in Paradise and promised an existence of eternal perfection—with one condition: They were not to eat the fruit of one particular tree in the Garden. Tragically, through a series of deceptive actions, the first couple found themselves expelled from Paradise.

To begin with, the serpent deceived Eve by attempting to blur the distinction between a divine order and a friendly piece of advice. (My father liked to remind me that Moses didn't come down from Mount Sinai carrying two stone tablets inscribed with the Ten Suggestions.) "Has God really said that?" The serpent beguiled her, and Eve listened to him. The woman went on to mislead her husband, who also chose to give in to temptation. The next layer of deception in this story came as these two attempted to deceive their Maker by passing the blame first to each other, then to the tempter. Adam blamed Eve, Eve blamed the serpent, and the serpent didn't have a leg to stand on. Seriously, though, why does telling the truth seem so difficult when stretching the truth comes so easily?

When God confronted Adam about his and Eve's disobedience, Adam turned to his wife and said, "I wouldn't be in this mess if it weren't for her!" Not wanting to take the blame, Eve offered an alibi of her own: "Well, if it hadn't been for this serpent, I wouldn't have done what I did," she said.

Of course God cannot be deceived, and He wasn't this

43

time. Adam and Eve, despite their excuses, were guilty of disobedience and were cursed because of it. It was at that point in human history that death came into the picture.

All of humankind has been living under that curse ever since.

We've seen some of the consequences of deceptive speech and actions. What motivates us to speak deceitfully? Why do we find it necessary to lie or twist the truth? Why do we tend to present the facts in a way that unfairly or deceitfully benefits us?

We should know better. There is something inside each of us that tells us that deceptive words are wrong, no matter what the circumstances. We know there is no excuse for willful deception, but at the same time there is a part of us that makes deceit a part of our very being.

One of the main causes of caving in to the giant named Deception is our own fear. Often when we lie it's because we fear the outcome of telling the truth. We lack the courage to face the consequences; perhaps we believe that we will lose our advantage if we speak forthrightly about our shortcomings or errors. We can see fear demonstrated in the story of the first humans, who tried—unsuccessfully—to cover their tracks after disobeying God in the Garden of Eden. Both of the first humans lied because they feared the repercussions that the truth might bring them. Of course, the destructive consequences came to pass despite Adam and Eve's futile attempts to protect themselves from their just due, death. The wages of sin are always death.[4]

We can also fall into deception because of simple greed for material or monetary gain. I spoke to you earlier about the giant named Discontent. He is a giant who will stop at nothing when it comes to satisfying our lust for more, and he is oh-so-good at using the greed in our hearts to motivate us to speak deceptively. I want to tell you that deceitfully gotten material wealth will never satisfy you, but will only make your lust for more stronger and stronger, to the point that it will consume you. When that happens, your possessions will own you, rather than the other way around. The giants named Discontent and Deception will gang up on you, pressuring you to lie—and then to justify your deception—to protect what you fear you might otherwise lose.

Our own anger also motivates us to use deception to "get even" with someone who has done us wrong. We do that by attempting to damage the offender's reputation with partial truths or outright lies. False words spoken out of bitterness can have the desired effect of damaging those they are aimed at. But speaking those kinds of deceptive words is like drinking poison and waiting for the other person to die: It may hurt your enemy, but eventually it will destroy you.

Finally, I want to talk about the selfish pride that can lurk within all of us, moving us into the path of the giant named Deception. Pride motivates us to use deception because we feel the need to build ourselves up in the eyes of the world around us. Friends, let me put this simply: Pride kills! Pride is at the center of so many of our shortcomings, and that includes our tendency to use deceit to get what we want.

You may examine how you speak and believe you've never given false testimony or spread a false report. Maybe you have always been careful to make sure your words were truthful. But I want you to think about something for a minute. The giant named Deception has several powerful weapons at his disposal, and they include deceit (outright lying), gossip (speaking about others in a harmful or malicious way, or listening when others do it), and flattery (complimenting or praising someone with impure, selfish motives).

Ask yourself if you've ever spoken a half-truth or twisted truth in order to gain an advantage. Ask yourself if you've ever engaged in malicious gossip about your neighbor. Ask yourself if you've ever spoken in a flattering way to someone to get what you wanted. If you've engaged in any of these things, then you've spoken deceptively.

When we look at all these things, we are led to one conclusion: We must conquer the giant named Deception, and we must do that by first disarming him, by taking from him the weapons he uses within us.

G ossip and slander are devastating weapons wielded by the giant named Deception. We can damage someone by spreading falsehoods about that person. We can betray others with gossip when we speak that which was told to us in confidence. Gossip destroys reputations, poisons friendships, and keeps arguments and quarrels that should have died alive, thriving, and growing.

How do we define gossip? What is the line between legitimately telling the truth about someone and maliciously attempting to attack someone's character or record?

Relaying information—even the most negative information—about your neighbor isn't necessarily gossip. There are times when it is just and proper to communicate negative facts about your neighbor. The key is in your motivation for conveying those facts. Your motives determine whether information you convey about others is constructive information or destructive gossip.

For example, suppose I knew a merchant who has been involved in unscrupulous business practices or whose merchandise is of poor quality. In that case I would be justified in relaying that information, in order to protect others from becoming victims. But I would be very much in the wrong if I told people that a certain businessman is dishonest or sells poor quality merchandise because I want to hurt that person, his reputation, or his business for my own advantage.

Gossip destroys a person's reputation, and that is no better than destroying his or her property—a crime according to our law. It is, in fact, verbal vandalism.

We are often motivated by greed or selfish ambition to gossip about others. We want what another person has—his business, his riches, his status—so we tear him down to build ourselves up. We may do that by spreading untruths about someone, but we can also do it by presenting the truth in a deceptive light.

While people spread some gossip just to gain an advantage, some gossip is nothing more than the result of meanness or a desire to get even with someone for a real or perceived wrong.

For example, I recently learned of a feud between two of my palace guards, Raban and Jabesh. These men had developed quite a dislike for each other, and it had a negative impact on their work performance. Instead of setting aside their differences and working together for the good of the kingdom, they did everything they could to tear each other down. Each sought to have the other fired, and he didn't care what it took to do it.

These two guards took turns on alternating days keeping the logbook of the attendance and performance of everyone in the palace command. Jabesh was prone to drinking a little too much wine, and one day when he came to work intoxicated, Raban joyfully noted in the logbook, "Jabesh reported for duty drunk today."

A few days later, it was Jabesh's turn to keep the log. Seething with anger over what Raban had reported about him earlier, he wrote, "Raban reported for work sober today." It was a truthful notation, but it was written with harmful intent. The implication was that Raban's sobriety was a rarity. Both of these men were wrong for doing what they did. They wrote the things they did about each other for one purpose only: to harm each other. If you aspire to have the "tallest building" in town, make certain that you concentrate on constructing your own rather than tearing someone else's down.

If you want to be a true and lasting success, you must never make use of the cruel weapon of gossip, and that includes making sure you never receive gossip from another.

Maybe you see yourself as innocent of the crime of gossip. Maybe you can't remember the last time you spoke ill of another for no legitimate reason. But let me ask you, have you ever listened to gossip? Have you ever received an unfavorable report about someone, the sole purpose of which was to do damage to that person?

In our system of law, receiving stolen goods makes you an accessory to robbery. In light of that, I tell you that receiving gossip makes you a participant in that sin. When you listen to gossip, when you refuse to tell the person "I don't need to hear this," but instead listen in, you are as much a gossip as he is. Our duty as upstanding citizens is to report a crime when we know about it, not to help it along. Listening to gossip makes us accessories to the crime. Listening to it enables the gossiper and fans the flames of gossip.

It is no compliment to you or your character when someone assumes you will lend an ear to negative reports. Don't just refuse to speak gossip; refuse to hear it. When someone tries to use your ear as a receptacle for the verbal garbage of gossip, resist with all your strength.

When someone brings gossip to your ear, don't just refuse to hear it. Ask the source of the gossip questions such as, "Have you checked this out and do you know it to be true? Have you brought this up to the person you are about to speak to me about?"

Many times, when someone has brought me morsels of gossip, I've challenged that person to verify not just the truthfulness of the words, but also his reasons for bringing them to me. You know what happens more often than not? That person backs off of his story.

There is never a circumstance where gossip is a good thing. It is poisonous communication that can never build up someone, but only destroy that person.

Stay away from gossip in any form! Decide that you will be known for exchanging words that build up rather than tear down.

I don't believe there are many—if any—people who haven't at some point spoken deceptively or engaged in gossip of some kind. But if you search your heart and examine your conscience and find that you speak with complete truthfulness and without a hint of gossip, then I want you to think about another form of deceptive talk: flattery.

Flattery can also be identified by our motivation. Flattery never takes into account its object, only what the flatterer can get from that person. It is good to praise people for their accomplishments, and it's fine to voice our admiration for someone's status. But when we praise someone with false, selfish motives, when we heap compliments on someone so that he will give us something we want, then we are engaging in flattery.

As the king of Israel, as the richest man in the world, as someone who has accomplished so much, I've learned to recognize flattery when it's directed my way. I've learned to recognize the false, dishonest motives of those who insincerely offer words of admiration and praise only because they want something from me.

I've realized that flattery, while it may not be an outright lie, is a deceptive form of communication and something I won't honor. It is using what may be a truth and twisting it so that we can get what we want. We need to stay away from flattery and make sure that the complimentary words we speak to others are spoken with pure hearts, hearts that are not trying to see what we can get from another person.

Speak words of kindness—to your friends, to your family members, to your business associates—but speak them only to bless those you come in contact with and not to get something from that person.

How do we defeat this giant named Deception? How do we train ourselves to keep our words honest in every way? How do we make sure that we don't entertain lies, half-truths, gossip, or flattery?

Here are some suggestions that can help you defeat this giant once and for all.

First of all, don't allow yourself the luxury of dressing up deceit in any form that makes it seem acceptable. In other words, call deception *deception*. Don't refer to untruths using expressions such as *white lies* or *half-truths*. Speak the truth, the whole truth, and nothing but the truth when you talk. Remember, a half-truth is always a whole lie.

When you are considering speaking negatively about another, stop and think about what you are about to say. First of all, ask yourself if what you are about to say is the absolute truth. If it isn't, keep it to yourself. Then ask yourself why you are considering repeating on this information, whether there is any real benefit to speaking it, or if you are trying to hurt the person you are talking about. If there is no benefit to what you want to say—and I mean benefit to all those involved, not just to your personal agenda—don't say it. Above all, make sure you are speaking this information out of a heart that wants to do what is best for all involved.

When you are considering speaking well of someone to his or her face, stop and think about your motives. Are you saying what you are saying to build up that person, to bless him or her? Is the benefit of what you are saying—outside of that very real inner blessing you receive for speaking kind, uplifting words to another—all his? If you find that you are complimenting another with selfish motives of seeing what you can get from him, don't do it.

Finally, count the cost of your words. Think about what you lose when you deal deceptively with those around you, in both word and action. Think long and hard about the advantages of speaking truthfully in every way.

Our fallen human nature makes it easy for us to rationalize our use of deception—including outright lies, twisted truth, gossip, or flattery. After all, we reason, if using these things helps us avoid pain or inconvenience, or if they give us even a little advantage in our business dealings, then why not? Whom are we hurting if we bend the truth a little? In fact, maybe it will end up benefiting both parties.

While we may attempt to rationalize our use of misleading and deceptive words, we can never justify this practice. It is wrong in the eyes of God and in the eyes of those around us to engage in deceit. And in a very real sense it's not a sound way to build a successful life.

I have learned that in the long run there is much greater reward to being a person of integrity—that when you deal untruthfully with others, it is only a matter of time before your lies are found out.[5] I also want to tell you—even as the richest man in the world—that I would rather lose every-thing I have to keep my conscience clean than have all these riches knowing that I've gained them by being deceptive.[6]

If you are considering dealing deceptively with anyone— a friend, a family member, a business associate—in order to gain in earthly riches or to advance your agenda, think again and don't do it. You're not gaining ground; you're losing it— in more ways than one.

Speaking deceptively may give you temporary benefits and advantages, but in the long run it just isn't worth it. If you want a happy, content, successful life, you will need a clean conscience, a conscience free of deceit of every kind. Then the only one "lying" will be the enemy named Deception—he'll be lying flat on his back as you stand over another conquered giant, holding the sword of truth heaven-ward in victory.

CHAPTER FIVE

THE SELFISH GIANT: DISREGARD

I want you to meet two different men, both of whom I know well. Men of extraordinary earthly achievement, they are both exceptionally wealthy. Both of these men live very comfortable lives because of their wealth. They both have beautiful homes and employ dozens of paid servants. Both own huge tracks of the most productive land, large herds of the highest quality animals, and stables filled with the finest horses. Of course, they both have all the money they could ever need or want.

But there is one huge difference between the two, and this difference has to do with the next giant I want to talk to you about.

One of the men is the picture of generosity. He pays his servants well, and he gives freely to help feed, clothe, and house those who aren't blessed with the material wealth he has. He regularly brings his tithes and offerings to the temple for God's work in our nation. Not only does this man give, he gives cheerfully. He *enjoys* giving of his wealth. To him, helping his servants to afford a comfortable life, feeding the poor around him, and seeing God's work go forward is blessing enough.

When people talk about this generous man, they use words such as *kind, humanitarian, giving,* and *benevolent.* Naturally, he's very well liked and admired in the community.

The other man is every bit as wealthy as the first, but he's anything but generous with his material blessings. Despite his extensive wealth, he's stingy when it comes to paying his staff, and he rarely helps the truly needy people around him. When it comes to bringing tithes to the temple, this man does it, but with a grimace on his face. This man, although he's been blessed with exceptional material wealth, lives a life of disregard for anyone's needs but his own.

When people talk about the second man, they speak in terms of his wealth and his accomplishments. But missing from their talk is the kind of praise the first man receives because of his generosity. Not only is this man not the object of love within his community, he is in fact despised in many circles because of his stinginess.

Okay, look at these two men, then tell me: Which one of them do you think is the happiest and most blessed in every aspect of his life? Which of these men is the most fulfilled in his work life, his family life, and his personal relationships? Which of these men is most loved and respected in his community?

Obviously, the first man is a truly blessed, happy man. The other man, however, despite his riches, has a hollowness about him that is obvious to all who know him. It's hard to come in contact with him and not walk away believing that there is something missing in his life.

This is all because the second rich man has been defeated by the next giant I want to talk about, the giant named Disregard.

My father used to tell me that good things come to those who give generously.[1] Indeed, I've seen in my own life that God loves giving prosperity to those who give freely,[2] that He blesses the man who doesn't cling too tightly to his money.[3]

When I spoke to you earlier about the giant named Discontent, I told you there was nothing inherently wrong with working hard to create material wealth, that it is fine to have ambition. But I warned against making the acquisition of material wealth the center of your life. I warned you not to allow yourself to fall into the trap of loving or serving money or material goods.

When you allow yourself to fall into those things, you have been defeated by the giant named Discontent. And as long as you are losing a battle with Discontent, you can count on Disregard to join in the fray. When the giant named Disregard goes to war with us, he more often than not enlists the giant named Discontent as his ally.

The giant named Disregard wants us to cling tightly to what we have earned—to what God Himself has generously given us. He defeats us by getting inside our heads and telling us that we don't have enough for our own needs, that we just can't afford to give to others. He takes us down by convincing us that if we give to eternal causes, then we'll be shorted and won't be able to pay our own way in the here and now.

There is something inside so many of us that makes it difficult, in some cases impossible, to part with our money for the good of others and even for God Himself. There is some part of our fallen nature that keeps us from enjoying the blessings we receive when we learn to give freely and joyfully.

Tell me, do you see yourself in what I've been saying here? Do you find it difficult to be generous to others, even the neediest among us? Do you struggle with giving cheerfully to God's work as He has instructed you to do? If so, then I can tell you that the giant named Disregard is squeezing the life out of you. In that case, no matter how rich you are, you are being robbed of true happiness, fulfillment, and blessing.

I have in my own life come to the conclusion that all the riches I own are in and of themselves meaningless unless my heart is filled with true peace, joy, and satisfaction. And I can't fully enjoy these things when I am stingy with what has been divinely appointed to me. On the other hand, when I am generous, God blesses me in what I have. Only then can I find true peace, joy, and satisfaction.[4]

My father once told me, "Solomon, though we are rich, we must not place our trust in our money, which will one day be useless to us. We must use our money to do good for those around us and to further the purposes of our God. We should be happy to give to those in need, to share with others what God has given us. When we do this, we will store up real, lasting treasures for ourselves. In the long run, this will prove to be the only wise, safe investment we could have made."

In the presence of true generosity, the giant named Disregard will be defeated on the spot. But how do we make use of the weapon of generosity? How do we take on an attitude—a heart condition, as some would put it—of giving?

I'd like to take some time now to talk about that, and I'd like to start off by talking about the principle of stewardship.

A mindset of generosity must begin with the realization that God has given us everything we have—our material riches, our power, our gifts and talents—and that He holds us accountable for how we use those things. Furthermore, it's the realization that God holds ultimate ownership over *everything,* and that includes all we have.

Lay hold of this truth, friends! Whether or not you acknowledge it, without the blessing of the generous hand of God Himself, you have nothing. Without that hand of blessing, you *are* nothing! And when God chooses to bless you, He expects you to use those blessings—material and otherwise—to do the things He wants done.

Does this mean we are to take vows of poverty? Does it mean we should give everything we have to the poor and needy and move into a cave? No! If it did, then I, as an extremely wealthy man, would have no room to talk to any of you about this. It simply means that our first priority, whether or not we are wealthy, is to use our resources in a way that reflects God's ultimate ownership of those things.

This is what I mean when I use the word *stewardship* when talking about how we handle our material wealth. And once we yield to the reality that we are not owners but merely temporary stewards of all that we have, we can then adopt an attitude of excitement about prioritizing life with eternity in view.

When you accept the bottom-line truth that all you have truly belongs to God, you will be freed to use your wealth in a way that is pleasing to Him. And I believe that when you do that, God will bless you with, among other things, additional wealth. But more than that, when you give freely of what you have, God will bless you with true happiness, joy, and fulfillment.

Perhaps you are in a position today where you don't know what you have to offer as far as material generosity. Maybe you don't have a lot to give, but I want you to know that there is no surer way of receiving blessings than by being a generous distributor of that which has been entrusted to you. Faithfulness with little prepares us to be rulers over much.

Let me illustrate this point. Let's say that you have two sons, and one day you decide to give each a large, equal amount of money from your bank account. You tell them that the following month you will increase the amount given them if they can meet certain conditions. "I want you to give one dollar out of every ten I give you to the work I'm trying to do," you tell them. "And after that I want you to use the remaining amount to give generously to the needy."

Let's say that one of the sons, showing total disregard for you, *your* money, and your instructions regarding how it is to be distributed, grabs the money and spends every cent on himself. Not only that, instead of giving the 10 percent you told him to give back, he clamors for more. The other son, however, thanks you for what you have given him, uses it wisely, and is sure to give back the 10 percent you told him to. He also gives generously and selflessly from the remainder to feed, house, and clothe those not as fortunate.

Let me ask you, which of these sons brought you greater joy and blessing? Which proved himself worthy of an increase the following month? I assert that the one who gave the 10 percent, then gave generously above and beyond, would be the one who received the greater blessing the following month. And I think you would agree that any father would feel cheated by the stingy son, the one who spent his money on himself.

Friends, the same is true of our Creator.

He comes to us giving generously, and when we are generous in kind, He pours out on us even more generosity. When we give, He gives more back to us because we have shown ourselves to be wise stewards. But when we choose to hold within a tight fist what He has given us, we will not only lose that initial blessing; we will rob ourselves of a further blessing.

We rob ourselves because we have robbed God. We have disregarded the fact that what God has "loaned" to us is rightfully His. The law of sowing and reaping is just as real as every other divine principle. It works every time. We simply have to decide whether it will work for us or against us.

If we are going to conquer the giant named Disregard, we must develop our "weapon" of generosity the way a good soldier develops his swordsmanship skills, with practice, practice, practice.

Conquering the giant named Disregard means understanding that you cannot serve two masters—namely, God and money. You will always be a servant to something, and if you do not serve God and regard what He has given you, you will become a servant to your money.

I serve God with all that I am—my words, my kingdom, my wealth. But I can tell you that I know a little something about becoming a servant to earthly riches. I know that when you place your earthly treasures at the center of your life, you will be defeated by the giants named Discontent and Disregard.

That, friends, is a quick road to despair, not a road to the promised land of lasting success.

Life brings plenty of tests, plenty of times when we can agonize over our situations. We are all faced with things we didn't plan for and don't want, often at the most inopportune moment. These are the times when we need to keep things simple, when we need to release to our Provider that which is rightfully His.

It's during these times in particular that we may be tested as to what is important to us, what we serve, and for whom we shall have the supreme regard.

Our forefather Abraham faced challenge when he was asked to give up the greatest gift he had ever received—his child of promise, Isaac. The Lord prompted Abraham to give up Isaac, the son he loved, on the altar. Abraham may not have understood why God wanted him to do such a thing, but he was obedient nonetheless. And when Abraham was found faithful to God, when God knew that he would not hold back his son, Isaac was spared.[5]

Abraham realized what we must also realize if we are to defeat the giant named Disregard: We are to serve God and God alone, and that there is nothing we shouldn't be willing to surrender to Him. Abraham selflessly gave up his son—though the very thought of it grieved him to the core of his being—just as we need to give up all that we have to bring glory to God.

God asks us to lay all our earthly assets—our money, our property, our possessions—on the altar for Him to use as He sees fit. When we do that, we will find the giant named Disregard not just defeated, but routed by generosity.

Be honest with yourself. Ask yourself some key questions about your struggle with Disregard. Do you consider yourself a generous person? And if you do consider yourself generous, do the facts back up your claim? Do all your financial accounts demonstrate a pattern of generosity? Have you truly laid all you have on the altar for God's use?

If you say that you are a generous person but your actions do not support your words, then you are being overtaken by the giant named Disregard. If you find yourself hesitating to give generously, then Disregard is blocking your pathway to lasting success.

Serve God with your wealth. Allow Him to have first place in all areas of your life, including the financial ones. Make Him the master of all you have and all you will have.

When you do that, you not only please Him; you give your earthly wealth eternal significance.

N one of us will take a single cent of our wealth with us when we pass from this life into eternity. All our land, all our homes, all our livestock, and all our money will stay here when we leave.[6]

But I believe that there is one way we can make our earthly wealth count in eternity, and that is to make generously giving to God's work a priority in our lives. Investing in people's lives now can yield a bountiful harvest in the future, and that has eternal significance we can't measure from this side of heaven.

Allow me to illustrate this eternal point using an earthly example. Suppose your country announced that it was about to convert its monetary system to the same one we use in Israel. Then suppose that legislation in your country had already been enacted so that this conversion to our monetary system would occur some time within the next twelve months. Obviously, when this conversion took place, the money you carry with you now would be rendered worthless.

But let us further suppose that in an attempt to make this upcoming transition fair to all citizens, neither nation released the official date on which the conversion was to take place. You knew with certainty that the conversion was going to take place during the upcoming twelve months, but you didn't know the actual day or hour of the conversion.

Knowing all that, what would be your best financial strategy?

Obviously, it would make sense to save just enough to get by for the next year, and convert the rest of your currency as soon as possible. That way, there would be no risk of losing everything you have on that future day of reckoning.

Well, my friends, this is exactly what is going to happen to your wealth when this life has been "converted" to the life to come. Unless it has been exchanged for eternal currency, it will be worthless when you stand before the One to whom we must all give account. It is the responsibility of each of us to store up treasures in heaven by making generous deposits here on earth.

This is bottom-line thinking, folks. It is the simple summarization of all I've told you about selfishly clinging to your wealth. It is the realization that without eternal perspective, our wealth—as comfortable and temporarily happy as it may make us—means nothing when all is said and done.

Each of us must begin today—through our generosity with those less fortunate, through our giving to the work God wants done—to convert our present wealth into the currency that is going to last beyond our lifetimes. It's the surest way to leave a legacy of lasting success.

And it will speak volumes to the next giant we battle about how serious you are when it comes to putting the needs of others high on your list of priorities—which is important, because this next monster is Disregard's evil twin.

CHAPTER SIX

THE UNFAITHFUL GIANT: DIVISION

My father's name was great in the nation of Israel. It still is.

As a very young man—one who had no experience in warfare—he did battle with a grave threat against the people of Israel. By now the whole world knows how my father's battle with Goliath the Philistine, seasoned after a lifetime of warfare, turned out. Wielding nothing but some stones and a simple slingshot, the eventual king of my people vanquished what loomed as a threat to Israel's very existence. From there, he went on to accomplish legendary things on the field of battle and as king of Israel.

With God's hand of blessing on him, my father fought and won many battles, the most famous of which was his battle with Goliath. But he later fought a battle with another giant, a giant who wanted to utterly defeat him.

This is the giant named Division, and he's a giant who can defeat us in our search for true success, for true happiness and peace. He wants to defeat us by pillaging all of our relationships—including our relationship with God.

Division lives within us, constantly tempting us to break our covenants—our promises—with other people and with God.

The giant named Division, like the other giants we have discussed, wants to destroy you, and in the process of destroying you he wants to destroy as many of your family members, friends, and business associates as he can.

I have lost count of the political and military careers I've seen destroyed, promising business careers I've seen doomed, and households I've seen devastated by acts of unfaithfulness.

Witnessing these things has made an impression on me, but in my heart and mind, none of them was as influential in my own thinking and life as my father's battle with the giant named Division.

Here is that story.

My father, David, was a great man and a great king of Israel, but there was one very dark period in his life, and it was the time following the moment he chose to violate his covenant with God and turn against one of his own soldiers who served King David with intense, unwavering faithfulness.

My father had everything he could have wanted or needed. He had many wives (in our culture, the quantity and quality of a king's harem reflects his power and prestige) and had fathered many children. Yet he desperately wanted what he shouldn't have, what he *couldn't* have: Bathsheba, who would later be my mother and who was married to another man when my father first gazed upon her beauty.

At that moment, the giant named Division had this otherwise powerful king right where he wanted him.

David violated the promise that he had made to God regarding moral purity by sinning with Uriah's wife Bathsheba, who became pregnant with his child. He then tried to cover up the affair by bringing the soldier Uriah home from battle to be with Bathsheba. David's hope was that when Uriah eventually learned that his wife was pregnant, after he had returned to the battlefield, he would believe the child was his own. When Uriah—out of intense loyalty to the king and out of respect for his fellow soldiers—refused to go home, David sent him to the front lines. He later died in battle.[1]

In short order, King David—this man who had so heroically and faithfully served his God and his nation, this man who had been so gloriously blessed by the hand of God, this man who had been referred to as a man after God's own heart[2]—had behaved unfaithfully to God by committing adultery and murder. David himself admitted that he deserved to die for what he had done.[3]

Prior to this circumstance, my father had been a great role model, exhibiting a near perfect balance of humility and confidence. When every other soldier trembled, he was fearless. When no one else would stand up and be counted, he was ready to do battle. But when the prophet Nathan confronted him about his actions and then announced, "David, you are the man who has sinned!" my father wilted. He responded the only way he could when faced with the truth: "I have sinned against the LORD!"[4]

Nathan told David that God had forgiven him and that

he would not pay with his life for what he had done. But the prophet also told him that there would be grave consequences for his sin, for his divided affections. Indeed there were. In addition to the death of my mother's late husband, Uriah, there was calamity in David's own household. Nathan's words proved to be true: The child born to David and Bathsheba died.

My father's grief over his sin took on a depth that so very few of us can understand. My father sinned grievously, but what made it worse for him is that it cost a good man his life. The death of such a faithful servant was difficult enough, but imagine the guilt and remorse you would feel if you knew beyond a doubt that you were responsible for that person's death, knew that you intentionally sent that person to his grave.

In his grief King David turned to God, who forgave him and brought him back into fellowship with Himself. Eventually, after a period of incredible darkness in his life, God restored my father.

But the consequences of my father's unfaithfulness followed him to his grave, serving as a reminder to me and to you of the importance of honoring covenants and keeping promises.

My father would have been the first to tell you that personal experience is a great teacher. Most of us who have engaged in an action that led directly to pain and sorrow choose never to engage in that action again. But there is a great lesson for all of us in what my father put himself through in his sin with my mother. It is the lesson of what can happen when we allow the giant named Division to reign in our lives, even temporarily.

King David never doubted that God had forgiven him of his sin.[5] Still, the memories of that failure—and they were horribly painful memories—stayed with him for the remainder of his life, reminding him and those who knew him of the importance of remaining faithful to one's covenants.

Of all the characteristics I admired about my father—and there were many—I would put his contrite heart at the top of the list. He was like any of us in that he could make mistakes and fall into sin. But he always knew when he was wrong, and he didn't make excuses or alibis for his sin. He showed me that when I have an opportunity to counteract a wrong I have a simple choice: I can make excuses or I can make progress, but I cannot do both simultaneously.

When I was quite young, my father wanted to write indelibly on my heart the importance of keeping covenants and of being faithful to God and His ways. He took me to the grave of my brother, who as a baby had died as a result of my father's sin. That day, as we stood next to my brother's tomb, my father said something I will never forget: "This, son, is the result of my unfaithfulness."

He then explained to me the lesson he had learned from that tragic sequence of events: "My son, it's better never to make a promise to God than to make one and not keep it, for He takes no delight in fools."[6]

I have many half-brothers and half-sisters, but the body of my only brother—the first son of David and Bathsheba, the one born out of their adulterous relationship—remains in his infant tomb as a stark reminder of the destruction that can come from breaking covenant relationships.

I n the divine order of things, we are covenantal beings. We make covenants in business associations, in friendships, in marriages, and in relationship with God.

When we hear the words *unfaithfulness* or *division,* our thoughts generally go to the breaking of the covenantal relationship of marriage. When we break our marital covenant, we break a promise made in front of our marriage partner, in front of human witnesses, and in front of God. When we do that, we in effect tell all those involved that our own desires are more important than keeping our vows and remaining faithful to our words and to our marriage.

Through Moses, God passed to the Israelites an absolute prohibition against adultery.[7] Clearly, God expected—and still expects—His people to be faithful to their marital vows. But marital infidelity is just one of many specialties of the giant named Division. There are many, many ways we can be unfaithful—to one another, to our own words, to our God.

When you break a promise to God or to another human, you have been unfaithful. If you violate any of God's statutes—not just His prohibition against marital infidelity—then you have been unfaithful to Him. When you go back on a business agreement because it's not convenient to fulfill your obligation, you have proven yourself unfaithful.

Integrity is very important to God because it is one of the attributes with which creatures can emulate the Creator. He expects us to be faithful in how we conduct our earthly relationships, including those of our birth families, our marriages, our friendships, and our business arrangements. He expects us to keep our word, to make sure that we always do what we say we will do. And, of course, He wants our undivided faithfulness to Him in every area of our lives[8]—not because He is a tyrant, but because He is the source of all good and perfect gifts.

While my father's restoration is an encouraging example of God's willingness to forgive, it also stands as a warning. It shows us that there are great consequences to be paid for allowing the giant named Division to hinder us from remaining true to God and His ways.

My father knew all too well the consequences of straying from God's laws, and through him I saw what can happen when we are unfaithful to our covenants with Him.

Although acts of unfaithfulness don't always result in such extreme consequences as the ones my family suffered, there is always a price to be paid. Our acts and words of unfaithfulness *might* result in consequences as severe as the ones David reaped. They *can* result in the fracturing of relationships between humans or the relationship between man and God. But breaking a covenant by being unfaithful *always* costs us because it invariably brings guilt, shame, and devastation in its wake.

That, friends, is a bottom-line principle: When we don't keep our covenants, when we are unfaithful to our word and to the divine laws, we *will* lose the peace and happiness we need to be truly successful. And we also risk losing more than that—much more, in many instances.

In our culture, we talk about the principle of sowing and reaping. It simply means that for every one of our actions and words there is a corresponding consequence. And when we sow seeds of mistrust and Division, that is exactly what we will reap.

There are tremendous consequences when we lose to the giant named Division. If we allow this giant to get the upper hand, we will live lives filled with strife between us, our families, our friends, our business associates, and yes, between us and God.

Given the certainty of the consequences of unfaithfulness, why would anyone risk it? Why would anyone allow himself to be defeated by the giant named Division, knowing what it could cost him? I submit to you that it comes from that part of our fallen human nature that seeks to elevate our own selfish needs and desires above those of others, even those who stand to be hurt by our unfaithfulness.

We are often unfaithful to our covenant agreements because we want to bolster our egos. Sometimes we do it because we believe we can "get a better deal" elsewhere. (When you think about it, that is just what went through my father's head when he first saw the beautiful Bathsheba.) There is a fatal misconception that stolen water tastes sweeter than water from your own well. But oh, how bitter it ultimately proves to be. Sometimes we do these things out of greed or envy, and sometimes it's simply the gratification of fleshly desires.

My father would have told anyone that covenantal

Division isn't worth the consequences. So would I. When we are unfaithful in these things, we damage our relationships with people around us and with God. When that happens, we lose the peace and joy that can make us true successes in this life.

The price of Division is high, to be sure, and no right-thinking person would want to pay such a cost. But now I want to talk about the positive. I want to tell you about the benefits of living a life of faithfulness.

What do we gain by conquering the giant named Division? What are the benefits of taking the positive step of making integrity a way of life?

When we conquer the giant named Discontent, we claim victory over our unholy desires for more material wealth. When we vanquish the giant named Deception, we bring our words into subjection so that they relay the truth from pure motives. When we fell the giant named Disregard, we remove "self" from the thrones of our lives.

When we conquer the giant named Division, we become people of integrity, people who keep their commitments, and people who keep their word no matter what the personal cost. We become people who keep their vows—to God, to their families, to their friends, to their business associates.

In short, we live like covenant people.

I can tell you from personal experience that life is far better for the man who is known for his faithfulness. Such a person has a happier marriage and family life, more fulfilling friendships, and more profitable business relationships. When we prove ourselves faithful, when we show ourselves to be people of integrity, we earn the respect of those around us. We are admired and loved by our family, trusted by our peers, and depended upon by our friends.

How does that work, you ask? It's the simple fact that those whose lives demonstrate covenant faithfulness are seen as more trustworthy in every area. People value faithfulness. The one who is faithful in how he lives is valued in friendships, in business relationships, and in marriage.

Think about that for a minute. No society builds monuments to men who aren't faithful to their agreements. Soldiers who violate the trust of fellow soldiers are executed as traitors. Merchants who violate contracts are run out of business or thrown into prison as frauds. Friends who violate the trust of supposed friends will sooner or later disqualify themselves from the blessedness of lasting friendships. And spouses who break their covenant agreement sign the death warrants for their marriages, often shattering entire households.

I can say with certainty that God blesses those who live lives of faithfulness. I can tell you that such a person finds true contentment, fulfillment, and happiness.[9] The Lord shows His faithfulness to the one who is faithful to Him[10] and guides that person's steps.[11]

Isn't all of this worth whatever effort may be required to honor your covenants and to fulfill your agreements?

THE UNFAITHFUL GIANT: DIVISION

If you want to achieve true greatness, if you want a life of real happiness and blessing, then you will need to become very serious about your battle against the giant named Division. That means keeping your covenants—with other people and, most importantly, with God.

Defeat this giant by honoring your covenants, by staying true to your word, and by keeping all your promises. Beat him by devoting yourself to unbending integrity in all transactions and relationships. Start by renewing—or beginning—your covenant relationship with God, then with all the people in your life: your family, your friends, your business associates. Remember that keeping your covenants might cost you—in terms of personal gratification, in terms of financial gain, in terms of recognition—but it is worth the price you pay.

When you keep your covenants with God and with men, when you faithfully keep your promises, the giant named Division is rendered powerless. You will then be living a life of faithfulness, and a life of faithfulness is one that leaves a blessed legacy.

The alternative? Well, remember my father's tragedy. When he took the giant named Division too lightly, the giant we'll be discussing next seized the opportunity to further manipulate him into committing evil of the highest order. It's scary to think what could happen to any of us if we give this next giant even the slightest entryway into our lives. He's bad news.

CHAPTER SEVEN

THE
CRUEL GIANT:
DESTRUCTION

It was a pivotal moment in the history of the nation of Israel, some believe *the* pivotal moment. It was the point when God's chosen people faced utter destruction, the point when it was time for someone to stand up and be counted.

Israelite soldiers—men who had seen their share of warfare—stood back in terror as day after day, week after week, the giant Goliath taunted them, sarcastically challenging them to find just one who had the courage to come out and fight like a man. "This day I defy the ranks of Israel!" the Philistine roared. "Give me a man and let us fight each other."[1]

In retrospect, it's not hard to understand the Israelites' fear. It's a serious understatement to say that Goliath was imposing. He was an awesome warrior who stood more than nine feet tall, and he was full of angry bloodlust. He had been a fighting man since his youth, and he had killed many, many men. Death was what he lived for.

Goliath had issued his challenge. He wanted a fight, and he wanted to destroy Israel's finest soldier right there in front of King Saul's army, then take the Israelites into slavery. There was no turning back for Israel now. Someone had to step up and conquer the Philistine giant or the entire nation of Israel would bow to foreign domination.

Only one man—a boy, really—stepped forward to do battle with what appeared to be an insurmountable foe. David, just a shepherd boy with no experience in battle at the time, went to King Saul and volunteered to fight Goliath. At first King Saul wasn't confident of David's ability to do battle with the giant, but David bravely assured the king that he could fight and win. After all, David told Saul, he had single-handedly killed ferocious animals in defense of his flock, so he knew he could defeat the Philistine.

Finally the king relented and sent David to face Goliath. "Go, and the LORD be with you," Saul told him.[2]

I have to wonder what the witnesses that day thought as they saw the young shepherd step up to do battle with a man who was not only well over twice his size, but who was also well armed and highly skilled in hand-to-hand combat. David, on the other hand, approached the giant wearing no armor and bearing no sword, his only weapons a sling and some rocks he'd learned to use while tending his father's sheep.

Imagine how that must have infuriated the Philistine! A mere shepherd boy standing before Goliath, taking him up on his challenge to fight to the death to determine the destiny of Israel. This was an insult to the giant, and he responded with hostility. I imagine that at that moment, an enraged Goliath wasn't thinking about simply defeating my father. No doubt he wanted to make a lasting statement with his victory over the boy. He wanted not only to destroy any threat from the army of Israel, but also to make sure that no one would even think of challenging him again. More than simply wanting to finish David off, this ungodly Philistine wanted to punish him for even daring to stand up to such a legendary warrior.

I know from the official record that Goliath showed utter contempt when he looked down upon the youngster who would one day brilliantly and courageously lead our people, the Israelites, in war against all our enemies. "Am I a dog, that you come at me with sticks?" Goliath bellowed, then cursed David by his gods. "Come here, and I'll give your flesh to the birds of the air and the beasts of the field!"[3]

In short, Goliath wanted to utterly destroy David and all that he stood for.

This is what destruction is all about. It's not about simply inflicting damage on your enemies. It's about making certain they never cross you again, about making certain they are no longer a "threat." It's about making your enemies subservient to you, about striking such fear into their hearts that they will never again oppose you.

These are the goals of the next terrorist, the giant named Destruction.

The giant named Destruction motivates us to destroy those who stand against us, those with whom we are angry, those we envy, those we resent. He taunts us as brazenly as did Goliath when he challenged Saul's army to send out a worthy opponent. This giant mocks us as foolish for regarding others' welfare above our own and challenges us to take what we may consider matters of justice into our own hands.

There is some fallen part of human nature that makes this giant's job easier. Instead of rejoicing with others when they excel, we become jealous. Instead of celebrating with them when they are honored, we show resentment. Instead of forgiving our enemies when they wrong us, we want to get even.

That's the effect when the giant named Destruction infects us with his poison.

Human history, including that of my people's culture, is full of examples of those whose lives were dominated by Destruction. I'm not proud of the fact that the history of the Israelites includes many instances of anger, jealousy, and resentment that moved men and women toward the destruction of their enemies.

We can see this sad aspect of human nature in the first recorded instance of physical murder. Adam and Eve's first son, Cain, killed his brother Abel out of anger and resentment. Cain was angry that his offering to God was not received with favor, while his brother's offering was. The consequences of Cain's sin were severe—he was banished from God's presence.[4]

Joseph, the favorite son of Jacob and the one whose future held the greatest destiny, was despised by his brothers. Their jealousy stemmed from the dream God gave to

Joseph revealing his call to leadership. Joseph's brothers originally plotted to kill him, but at the insistence of one of the brothers they decided instead to sell him into slavery and tell their father that wild animals had attacked him. While they didn't physically kill Joseph, their intent was clear: They wanted to destroy their brother by taking him away from what God had called him to do.[5]

But if God is for you who can be against you? Like Abel and Joseph before him, my father was the object of sibling jealousy and resentment. This after he heroically battled and defeated Goliath the Philistine, something none of the Israelite soldiers had the courage to do. Instead of appreciating him his brothers abhorred him. When you begin to soar with the eagles, the attention you command will infuriate anyone who lacks the courage to soar with you.

David had approached the battlefield with confidence, knowing that God had called him to this fight. "You come against me with sword and spear and javelin, but I come against you in the name of the LORD Almighty, the God of the armies of Israel whom you have defied," David told the enraged giant. "This day the LORD will hand you over to me, and I'll strike you down and cut off your head. Today I will give the carcasses of the Philistine army to the birds of the air and the beasts of the earth, and the whole world will know that there is a God in Israel."[6]

You all know by now that my father made short work of the giant and that the armies of Israel went on to rout the Philistines. As the Israelite army returned home from this miraculous victory, women sang songs proclaiming, "Saul has conquered thousands and David tens of thousands."[7]

You would think that King Saul, having just witnessed the salvation of his nation, would have joined in the celebration. But instead, Saul's jealousy against David, the young man who had so faithfully and heroically served the kingdom, caused the king's heart to burn hot with anger to the point that he tried repeatedly to kill the anointed future king of Israel.[8] Jealousy had given the giant named Destruction a foothold in Saul's divided heart, and he responded by trying to put an end to the dawn of a great kingdom.

Cain, Joseph's brothers, and King Saul—as well as many others too numerous to list here—all responded out of jealousy and resentment and let Destruction rule how they responded to their situations. Consequently, they occupy places of eternal infamy in the history of my people.

I would assert today that in the realm of human behavior, there is nothing all that unusual or shocking in the way these men responded to the success of their enemies.

My father used to put it this way: "Solomon, only a handful of people will ever genuinely delight in your achievements." Many of the others, I am sad to report, find it necessary to try to destroy you.

Friends, none of us are above behaving—in different manifestations—the way Cain, Joseph's brothers, or King Saul did. There is something inside each of us that wants to get even if we don't get our own way.

It might be shocking to you to think of literally killing your enemy or rival. Maybe you'd never even consider inflicting physical damage upon another person. But there is another kind of destruction I want to focus on today, the kind brought about through hurtful words and actions, the kind that destroys the reputation, the self-esteem, or the well-being of our enemies.

How many of us have tried to kill our enemies with words instead of spears? How many of us have attempted to destroy our adversaries using spiteful actions instead of swords? How many of us have attempted to defeat our rivals with gossip instead of a dagger?

Centuries ago, Moses handed down the law, which included the words, "You shall not murder."[9] Most of us, particularly those who obey God's laws, would never consider literally taking the life of another innocent human. But I believe there is more to this commandment than the prohibition of physical murder. I would assert that the spirit of this law condemns the destruction of another human in any way.

You don't have to literally end someone's physical life in order to destroy that person. In the eternal realm, it's as wrong to damage another person with hateful, spiteful words as it is to damage that person physically. In that sense it's as wrong to "kill" someone's self-worth or reputation with speech or attitudes as it is to literally murder that person with a weapon of wood or stone.

Civil authorities will never throw you into prison for wishing for the destruction of someone's business or family or even his very life. But that kind of thinking will bring you into another kind of bondage that is just as real as a physical prison.

When your life is ruled by hatred or spite toward others, you are living life with a giant weight strapped to your back. When you make efforts to destroy others with your words and actions, it is just a matter of time before you destroy yourself with those same words and actions. When we live by the sword we die by the sword.

It gets back to the principle of sowing and reaping, which I mentioned in an earlier session. When you sow destruction in the lives of others, you will reap the same from them. When you sow hatred and spite, they are what you will reap. Hatred and destruction have a way of dominating our lives. When these things become our source of motivation, it's not long before everything we do will be centered around making sure we "win out" over our enemies, rivals, and others we perceive to have wronged us.

I f you do not conquer the giant named Destruction with finality, he will destroy you. It is that simple. You cannot enter the promised land of lasting success while constantly looking over your shoulder for another and yet still another encounter with this enemy.

Destruction must be more than controlled if we are to enjoy true and lasting success; rather, he must be utterly destroyed. We must remove from our lives any hint of his influence, then we must slay him once and for all.

Make no mistake about it, when you have the giant named Destruction where you want him, he will plead for his life. He will bargain with you and try to convince you that he's really your ally, that you need him if you are to be successful in this competitive, cutthroat world. He will look you in the eye and tell you that if you don't have him, you'll be powerless against a world that would just as soon chew you up and spit you out as look at you.

But don't listen to his desperate lies and rationalizations. Don't believe one word Destruction utters as he begs you to let him live. Don't treat him as any kind of ally but as an enemy who, if he is not dealt a final blow, will come back and ambush you when you least expect it. Treat him as a disease that, if left to run its course, will destroy you from within.

Friends, this is one time when I would plead with you to show no mercy. When you purpose in your heart to conquer the giant named Destruction, you need to make it your goal not just to win the battle, but to destroy him for good.

My father was merciless when he defeated the Philistine. Indeed, mercy was not an option that day, as David knew that if he defeated Goliath in a fight but let him live, it would have been just a matter of time before this terror confronted the Israelites again—only angrier and more intent on gaining vengeance for his earlier defeat. Likewise, if you don't annihilate Destruction in your life, if you don't end his existence, you can be sure that he will come back at you later and attempt to destroy your marriage, your friendships, your business relationships, and your relationship with God.

H ow do we destroy the giant named Destruction? How do we take away his foothold in our lives so that we can end his existence? How do we first defeat this formidable foe, then administer a final death-blow?

The first question you must ask yourself as you endeavor to destroy Destruction is this: How willing are you to conquer this giant who poisons your relationships with others, harms people's reputations and self-worth, causes you anxiety and bitterness, and in the long run blocks you from entering the promised land of lasting success? And how important is it that you be completely and permanently free of this giant's influence?

It you are truly committed to conquering Destruction, then I have some steps for you to take—steps I have personally proven will give you the victory over this dangerous giant.

The effort to conquer this giant starts with changing your way of thinking about others, with realizing that every human being—even those you may consider your enemies, rivals, or competitors—has value in the eyes of God who created us all.[10] When you realize that the people around you are valuable creations of God, then you will be motivated from the heart to respond to them the way God responds to any of us: with kindness, goodness, gentleness, and forgiveness.[11] Understand that each of these spiritual fruits can coexist with justice. Judgment and mercy are not mutually exclusive.

I can tell you from my own experience that there is no

more fulfilling way to deal with others than by showing kindness and gentleness—even to those who have done you wrong.[12] On the other hand, I have found angry vengeance to be at best unsatisfying, and at worst personally destructive.

The second step in conquering the giant named Destruction is simply controlling your tongue. You must make it your practice to speak words of kindness to those around you—even those with whom you have conflicts. You must replace words of anger and revenge with words of love, tolerance, and forgiveness.[13] A gentle answer turns away wrath.[14]

My father used to tell me that our words reflect what is in our hearts. He would say, "Remember, son, out of the abundance of the heart the mouth speaks."[15] I have found that to be true; furthermore, deciding to speak kind words can also influence our hearts toward attitudes of love and forgiveness. In other words, when you speak words of kindness, your heart actually moves that direction for others. Maintaining those attitudes will slowly but surely bring destruction upon the giant named Destruction.

The final blow to this giant is to seek forgiveness for our murderous words, attitudes, and actions—from those we have sought to destroy, and from God Himself.

A wise man will always take the time to make amends for his sin against another person.[16] I know there is much value in humbling ourselves and in contritely approaching those we have wronged with our words and actions. When we do that, we repair relationships and soothe our own consciences.

Taking that one step further, I can tell you without question that divine favor rests on those who pray for changed hearts and who cooperate by turning from their destructive words and actions. If anyone is aware of the fact that murderers can be forgiven, it's me. My father, in an absolute abuse of power, ordered the death of my mother's former husband to cover up their adulterous affair and her resulting pregnancy. Eventually, God sent the prophet Nathan to my father; he pronounced harsh judgment upon King David.[17]

My father didn't make excuses for what he had done. Instead he humbly and genuinely pursued forgiveness. Although the consequences for his actions still lay before him, my father received not only forgiveness and restoration but also the message of hope that came from his experiences.

When King David first told me that God shows favor to those whose walk is blameless before Him and to those who do what is right, I was confused. I said, "Father, since our people are still eagerly awaiting the blameless One to come into the world, how could I possibly be blameless in His sight?"[18]

He smiled at me and said, "Solomon, what is impossible for man is possible with God.[19] He judges sin and then counts the repentant blameless. Someday He will bear our infirmities so that we may be healed. The poor shall be made rich and the blind will see through new eyes." Although I was just a boy at the time, I remember feeling secure and thinking, "If God is for me, who could be against me?"

The giant named Destruction may loom over you and me

the way Goliath towered over the shepherd boy. But like David, when we refuse to back down to Destruction's threats and face him in the power of God, we cannot lose. We become more than conquerors through Him who loves us!

Let that truth intensify your commitment to lead many others to the promised land of lasting success. We're halfway there! Five giants down…five giants left to be conquered.

CHAPTER EIGHT

THE UNGRATEFUL GIANT: DISHONOR

I will never forget the things my father said to me as his death grew near. King David, this brave, heroic man who had fought and won so many battles on behalf of his God and his people, called me to his side, looked me in the eye, and spoke with great conviction about how important it was for me to carry on our family's legacy of serving God and the nation of Israel.

"Solomon," he said, "be strong and show yourself to be a man. Observe what the LORD requires of you. Walk in His ways and keep His commands and requirements, as has been written in the Law of Moses. If you do that, you will be successful and prosperous in all you do and wherever you go."[1]

With that said, my father—who served gloriously as king of his people for forty years—entered eternity, leaving the throne as king of Israel in my charge.[2] But he left more to me than just a position of royalty. He also charged me with the responsibility of being the same kind of steward of the office that he was. He reminded me to make sure that I made our

God and His laws the center of my kingdom.

This was a deeply solemn charge my father laid on me, and there was no question in my heart or mind that I was going to do everything I could to honor my father's final request. On the day I took the throne as Israel's king, I knew I had an awesome legacy—not to mention a high calling from God Himself—to live up to. I also knew that there would be those who would struggle somewhat with the idea of serving under a new king.

I firmly believe that one of the big reasons I have been a success as king of my people and have been richly blessed in every way is because I honored my father and my mother in every area of my life.

In doing that, I have defeated in my own life the next wily enemy who lurks close to home, the giant named Dishonor. When I talk about dishonor, I'm referring to our inherent rebellion against authority. Rebellion's earliest manifestations are nearly always against our parents, the two people God utilized to bring us into this world.

I think it is sad that there is so little attention paid in most cultures to the command to honor mothers and fathers. Even now you may be sneering at the idea of truly honoring your mother and father, wondering what it could possibly have to do with productivity or peace or any form of lasting success in this life.

Before this session is done, I want to show you just how important it is that we honor the ones who at the very least gave each of us life, and I want to start by showing you how the giant named Dishonor cleverly works to defeat us in seemingly unrelated areas of our lives.

Like the other giants we have previously discussed and the ones we will identify later, Dishonor has many weapons at his disposal, weapons he uses ferociously and cruelly in order to torture us.

How does the giant named Dishonor do that and what weapons does he use in his attempts to weaken us?

Dishonor first minimizes the benefits of submitting to authority by causing you to focus your attention on what your parents weren't, instead of on what they are—that is, the ones God assigned to give you life. This giant wants you to focus on what your mother and father didn't give you and not on what they did. He wants you to focus on the negatives, on the things your parents did wrong in rearing you, and not on what they may have done right.

This giant poisons you by gradually filling your heart with ingratitude and discontentment; when your heart is running over with those things, there is no way that you can experience a genuine appreciation for submitting yourself to anyone else. "Why should I?" you find yourself saying. "They will only disappoint me." The giant named Dishonor, like the other giants we have discussed thus far, must be silenced because if there is one common thread in our discussion, it's that all of these giants want to destroy our effectiveness with our people. I don't think anyone could argue that conquering any one of these giants wouldn't in some way improve how we relate to our friends, neighbors, family members, and business associates.

I said in an earlier session that it is a mistake to measure our success and happiness by our financial or material blessings. The worth of a man's life is not in the abundance of his possessions. Sadly, too many of us have fallen into the trap of misinterpreting success and happiness, which has led to an overshadowing in our hearts and minds of the legacy we receive from our parents and, in turn, leave to our children. We place great value on the monetary inheritance we receive from our mothers and fathers, but we often tend to overlook the lasting things they pass on to us.

I can tell you from personal experience that such thinking is completely backward in the divine order of things. It is also a guarantee that that same destructive attitude will infect future generations.

Friends, I want to say it now: If you want to get an accurate measure of someone's accomplishments in life, then take a look at the legacy he has left for his children and for his children's children. If you intend for your children to honor their parents, you will have to model that attitude toward their grandparents. The student is no greater than the teacher.

My father passed on to me an incredible legacy. Yes, he passed on all the earthly riches, but more importantly, he passed on to me those things that will last not just beyond his own earthly existence, but beyond my own and my children's. He passed on to me the wisdom of all his years as king of Israel and as a man who, although he stumbled at points in his life, was a man after God's own heart. One of the many ways in which he exemplified greatness was to treat my grandfather, Jesse, with great respect.

It was that legacy I wanted to continue as I took the throne as the king of my people.

I n my culture, we hold our mothers and fathers in a high place of honor. That is with good reason. Centuries ago, Moses—the man God chose to deliver the Israelites from four hundred years of Egyptian serviture—descended from Mount Sinai with the law God Himself had given him. Within that law, the law that God's chosen people were to live by, were these words: "Honor your father and your mother, that your days may be prolonged in the land which the Lord your God gives you."[3]

In this context, the word *honor* literally means "to give glory to" or "to hold in high esteem" or "to value and treasure." In other words, when we give glory to those who brought us into this world, hold them in high esteem, and value and treasure them, then we can expect God to reward our obedience. His conditional promise for those who honored their parents was, "Your days will be prolonged in the land the LORD gives us."[4]

At this moment you might logically ask how honoring your parents could possibly make your life longer and more blessed. Well, in the divine order as laid out in the law of Moses, mothers and fathers play the roles of teachers of the sacred matters. They are commissioned by the law to diligently teach and encourage their children to love God and to live as He instructs them to live. They are admonished to never let their children forget God and the things He expects of them.[5]

Being a good parent—a father or mother who takes an interest in the physical, emotional, and spiritual aspects of his child's life, a parent who trains his child in the ways of

God—isn't easy. It is a noble calling that requires tremendous emotional investment, as well as a great expenditure of time and energy.

There are two differing yet interrelated responsibilities in God's instructions to parents and children. Moses recorded many instructions from God concerning parents' responsibilities to teach and nurture their children, and, as with the rest of the divinely inspired law, we are expected to live in obedience to those instructions. Furthermore, God drove home to His people the value He placed on parenthood when He decreed severe penalties for those who so much as cursed their parents.[6]

Clearly it is of utmost importance to God that we honor our mothers and fathers. It is equally clear that this is an avenue of His blessing.

At this moment you may be mentally acknowledging God's call for you to honor your parents, but at the same time there may be something inside you that resists full compliance with that command. More often than not, people who respond that way do so because they come from families with parents who didn't fulfill the responsibilities with which God had charged them.

What if that's true in your life? What if your parents didn't live up to their part of the bargain? What if your parents neglected to supply you with the teaching and nurturing you needed when you were growing up? What if they not only neglected their responsibilities but also made things worse through acts of verbal or physical abuse?

I'm not here to make excuses for any of your parents' shortcomings. I know there are many abusive and neglectful parents out there, many who don't teach their children the things they need to know in order to be truly successful in this life or in the life to come. There are many out there who did little more than bring their children into the world, then abandoned them to fend for themselves.

You won't be able to conquer all the giants you will face if you resist change regarding any one of them. The fact that your parents didn't meet their obligations to you does not relieve you of the responsibility you have to God in honoring your parents. It doesn't matter how well or how badly your parents handled caring for you when you were a child; they are still due honor simply because of their God-given office as the people who gave you life. You may say, "Well, I didn't ask to be born!" You're absolutely right; that wasn't your doing at all. It was God's idea. *You* are God's idea. If you like the idea, thank Him. If you don't like the idea, take it up with the Creator. Meanwhile, honor those—or their memory, if they're gone—who allowed you your first breath.

In most every society, the individual person has a certain say in the covenant relationships they enter into. For example, you choose whom you will marry and with whom you will enter into business relationships. However, there is one covenant relationship in which you cannot choose your partners, and it is that of who your parents are.

Given that fact, it is your responsibility—not that of either or both of your parents—to defeat with finality this giant named Dishonor.

Dishonor can be one of the easiest of the giants to bring

down, or he can be one of the most difficult, depending upon how much you choose to focus on your parents' "scorecard." I say that because I know that God requires us to honor our parents, but also because I realize that it's not always easy to honor imperfect human beings who make plenty of mistakes, including mistakes in how they raise us.

Nevertheless, if you aspire to true greatness, this giant must be defeated in your life. Let's look at some practical ways that we can fight this battle and win, even when we have parents whom we don't see as worthy of the kind of honor God says is due them.

The first, and most important, step in conquering the giant named Dishonor is to simply acknowledge your parents' position as your mother and father. This means that despite your mother and father's imperfect behavior—even the behavior they, for whatever reason, have not made amends for or even acknowledged—you should honor them as the two people God used to bring you into the world.

If it shocks you to hear me say that you owe your parents honor for simply giving you physical life, then look at it this way: If all that your parents had ever done was to give you life on earth—even if they had abandoned you immediately—then everything you have accomplished here would still be attributable to them. For that reason, you owe them the honor and God the thanks for giving you life.[7]

Still you may ask, "Why did God use *these* two people or *this* situation to bring me here? Couldn't He have done it using a more conventional family?" I will grant you that it's not easy—if it's even possible—to understand why God chooses to do things the way He does. But I can promise you one thing: If you will respond obediently to God's commandment to honor your mother and father, then He can bless you richly in relationships, since all healthy relationships are founded upon a proper respect for others.

Let me illustrate this point. When you walk into a courtroom, how do you address the person sitting at the judge's bench? You address him as "Your Honor," don't you? And does how you address the judge have anything whatsoever to do with his or her personality or character? Not at all! This judge may be unfair, harsh, and profane in his personal life, but you still honor him because of the position he holds.

It is to be the same way with your mother and father. No matter how they fall short in their roles as parents, no matter what kind of sin they took part in, no matter how neglectful—even abusive—they may have been, they are still due honor for their position as those who gave you life.

Please understand that honoring your parents' position doesn't mean that you don't acknowledge their mistakes and their sins. It doesn't mean that you accept actions that are, on all levels, unacceptable.

My father would never have expected me or anyone else who knew him to approve of his adulterous affair with Bathsheba. There is no way to justify the affair, no way to excuse what King David did that day. Just as my father did so many years ago, I acknowledged his moral failings and learned the lessons from them that I am supposed to learn.

My father fell short of God's standards of conduct when

he sinned with the woman who would become my mother. But God forgave, restored, and healed him when he turned to the Lord in humble repentance.

I have always honored my father and my mother—not for the circumstances that brought them together, and not for the circumstances that led to the birth of my brother or me, but for giving me life, for bringing me into an existence in which God has richly blessed me and allowed me to bless others.

Friends, remember this: When you forsake your feelings of anger or bitterness toward those who bring you into life, you also rid yourself of the ingratitude that always accompanies those feelings. And when you rid yourself of ingratitude, you begin to move toward achieving your goal of lasting, meaningful success.

Once we learn to acknowledge the unique position our parents hold in our lives, we can move on to the next step in conquering the giant named Dishonor. That step is learning to be grateful for what they have done for us—even if it's for nothing more than giving us life. This is essential if we are to ever fully develop an attitude of gratitude toward other authority figures in our lives, whether rulers or guardians or teachers.

I spoke first about acknowledging your parents' position as your lifegivers because I believe that it is impossible for many of us to truly honor our parents without first learning to be grateful for the gift of life, the gift that God used two people of His own choosing to give you.

Some of you come from homes where both your mother and your father took great care to train you up in the way

God wants you to go.[8] If that is the case in your life then you should be especially grateful to your parents. It was no small feat for them to do what they did for you, and they deserve high honor for that. Others of you, however, come from families where you were given little more than life. Those are parents who have not only neglected their God-ordained responsibilities to you but who have also missed out on the blessings that being a responsible parent can bring.

You can make progress in conquering Dishonor by taking the time to appreciate what your parents have done for you—whether it's in recognizing how they followed God's laws or in acknowledging that they gave you life.

When you start with that simple step, you will be amazed at how your grateful heart will pierce the evil heart of the giant named Dishonor. But if you stubbornly insist that any unresolved authority issues—parents or other-wise—won't keep *you* from being successful, I must warn you: The insatiable, profane, and counterfeit trio of giants you're about to meet is notorious for ganging up on people who laugh at Dishonor.

CHAPTER NINE

THE INSATIABLE GIANT: DIVERSION

I said earlier that there is nothing at all wrong with diligent, hard work as a means to accomplish great things in this world, even in the monetary sense. I'll take that a step further and tell you that hard work is a necessity if you are to achieve financial success and that laziness is a sure path to poverty.[1]

Simply put, God blesses us when we work hard, when we diligently perform the tasks we set out to do. This is how we earn earthly wealth honestly. If we desire to achieve great things in this world, if we want to earn monetary riches, then we'll need to work hard in whatever field we have chosen.

There is, however, a balance we must strike in this area of our lives if we are to be successful in the true and lasting sense. And in striking that balance, we must battle and defeat our next giant, the giant named Diversion. This giant wants us to make our work the very center of our lives, to the very point where we discount all other things, including our families, our friends, our health, and even our God.

He will sometimes cleverly substitute pleasure for work—in the financial sense—to ensure that we deviate from that which is most important. But whether we're working too much at our jobs or "working" too much on our hobbies, we are being tricked by the giant named Diversion.

In our quest for true and lasting success, it can be easy to fall into this kind of thinking. Our human logic tends to imply that if long hours of hard work are good, then *longer* hours of *harder* work must be even better. Simple reasoning tells us that if we work seven days a week, we'll accomplish more than if we work just six days and rest one day. That sounds like elementary mathematics, doesn't it?

I want to tell you emphatically that this isn't necessarily so. I know for a fact that when it comes to the amount of time we spend working at work, or "working" at avoiding work, there comes a point when we reap diminishing returns on our productivity. In fact, I believe that it is possible to actually *lose* some of what we've gained when we work too many hours in a week. And we don't lose just in the monetary sense, either. We also lose in our relationships with our families, with our friends, and with our God. When that happens, we have been blindsided by Diversion.

Without a doubt, this is not the way God intended it to be. In the divine order of things—as laid out in the laws the Lord passed to His chosen people through Moses—God arranged for His people to have a day of rest every week from their work, a day He named the Sabbath.

Here is what the law of God says concerning that holy day of rest:

> Remember the Sabbath day by keeping it holy. Six days you shall labor and do all your work, but the seventh day is a Sabbath to the LORD your God. On it you shall not do any work, neither you, nor your son or daughter, nor your manservant or maidservant, nor your animals, nor the alien within your gates. For in six days the LORD made the heavens and the earth, the sea, and all that is in them, but he rested on the seventh day. Therefore the LORD blessed the Sabbath day and made it holy.[2]

This divine principle covers each of us as individuals, but it also covers our families, our servants, alien workers, even our animals. Clearly it was important to God that we have a time of rest.

You may ask, "Why a Sabbath day? Why should God care if I wanted to work seven days a week for the rest of my life? Why does He want me to stop and rest one day of the week?"

Each of God's commandments is given with His glory and our benefit in mind. This commandment to honor the Sabbath is no exception. There are two fundamental reasons for the Sabbath. The first is that we are created with a need for rest and rejuvenation. The second reason for the Sabbath is that God wanted us to set aside a day where we could forget our earthly pursuits and concentrate our hearts and minds on spiritual development.³

Let's discuss the first purpose for the Sabbath—the inherent physical benefits.

God did not create humankind to work without ceasing. Rather, He created us with a built-in need to stop our work for a time of renewal for our bodies and minds. This is a natural order that has been divinely laid out from the very beginning of creation. The written account of that creation, as recorded by Moses, indicates that the Lord didn't just tell His people to honor the Sabbath, but that He Himself set the example.

The Lord worked six days to create all that we can see around us—the universe, the earth, and all the diverse creatures that inhabit this world, including humankind. When we look around us in any direction, we can see the awesome, wonderful work of God's creative hand.

When this awesome project of creation was completed, the Lord sat back, looked at it, and said that it was "good." Then, on that seventh day, He rested:

By the seventh day God had finished the work he had been doing; so on the seventh day he rested from all his work. And God blessed the seventh day and made it holy, because on it he rested from all the work of creating that he had done.⁴

He rested from the work. Does this mean that the Creator of the universe, the Lord of all, was worn out and needed to take a day off? Was God tired? Of course not. This was simply God's way of defining one aspect of humankind's earthly behavior. It was His way of establishing a divine order for how we would best function. He knew that as flesh-and-blood beings, each of us would need this time of rest.

Friends, it is a God-ordained law that hard work deserves a time of rest and renewal in order to encourage productivity. That is why God has commanded His people to take the seventh day and make it a day of rest, a day to be honored and set aside as holy.

This principle of rest is so important to the Lord that He insisted that the very earth the Israelites plowed and planted was to be given a time of rest:

> The LORD said to Moses on Mount Sinai, "Speak to the Israelites and say to them: 'When you enter the land I am going to give you, the land itself must observe a sabbath to the LORD. For six years sow your fields, and for six years prune your vineyards and gather their crops. But in the seventh year the land is to have a sabbath of rest, a sabbath to the LORD. Do not sow your fields or prune your vineyards. Do not reap what grows of itself or harvest the grapes of your untended vines. The land is to have a year of rest. Whatever the land yields during the sabbath year will be food for you—for yourself, your manservant and maidservant, and the hired worker and temporary resident who live among you, as well as for your livestock and the wild animals in your land. Whatever the land produces may be eaten.'"[5]

Indeed, just as the principle of rest can be seen in the human context, it can be seen in this principle of rest for the land. Farmers in my kingdom, men who know so well how to make use of the land God has given us to produce food for the people, have told me that it is highly beneficial for a plot of land to be left unplowed and unplanted for one year out of seven so that it can naturally rejuvenate itself, thus making it more productive when it is plowed and planted the following growing season.

Think about it for a minute: If the very land God created needs regular rest and rejuvenation, how much more do we as flesh-and-blood human beings need it?

I'd like to illustrate this connection between the human need for rest and the increase of productivity with a story about a very successful builder whom I know. This story demonstrates the practical value of a time of rest from one's work.

King Hiram of Tyre assisted in the building of the palace[6] and provided the kingdom with all the cedar and pine for the Temple, a project completed under my own kingship.[7] His story demonstrates the human need for regular rest and rejuvenation.

As a young man, Hiram had become quite an accomplished axman. He could produce more cut lumber than some of the most experienced foresters with whom he worked.

Hiram remembered one day when he was paired with another axman who was older but less experienced at working with wood. Their job that day was to split logs into boards, which were to be used in the kingdom. At the end of the first hour, Hiram noticed that he and his coworker had split an identical number of boards. Being fresh and full of energy because it was still the beginning of the day, both workers were producing at an impressive rate. But when that first hour was finished, Hiram left his work station to rest for a few minutes, get a drink of water, and have his cutting instruments sharpened.

Although Hiram was gone for only five minutes, the coworker pulled ahead noticeably in the number of boards split. But that didn't last long: Hiram quickly caught up with and then passed his coworker in the number of boards split. By the end of the second hour, Hiram had taken a noticeable lead over his partner. Again Hiram left to take a break from his labor to refresh himself and get his cutting equipment sharpened. When he returned, the two men's stacks of boards were roughly equal.

At midday both men stopped to eat, drink some water, and rest. That was the elder man's only break of the day. Hiram, on the other hand, had stopped working for five minutes every hour on the hour to rest his body and give his cutting implements a good sharpening.

As the day progressed, Hiram began to build a big lead in boards produced. When the foreman checked the men's production levels at the end of the day, he noted that Hiram had outproduced his partner considerably. In addition, the elder worker was completely exhausted. Although he was also tired from the day's work, Hiram still had energy left. Hiram's partner, his exhaustion surpassed only by his humiliation at being so greatly outproduced, wanted to know Hiram's secret. "You made me look very bad in front of the foreman today," he told Hiram. "How did you do it? I never said anything about it to you or to the foreman, but not an hour went by that you didn't desert your post and disappear into the woods on company time. I never left my post, yet you produced a great many more boards than I did. What's your secret?"

"Friend," Hiram replied, "I'm glad you asked me about this, because I want you to understand that when I left our work post I wasn't loafing. You see, I was taught long ago that a weary worker with a dull ax blade is no match for a refreshed worker with a sharp ax blade."

Hiram went on to explain to his coworker that by the end of the first hour of the workday, he noticed how much more effort it took to cut wood with a blade that had dulled considerably in just an hour's time. So instead of struggling to cut boards with a dull ax blade—which would have cut down his levels of production and energy—he took his ax to an ironsmith who had set up shop nearby. Each time the ironsmith sharpened his blade, Hiram explained, he had gone to a nearby stream, taken a long, cool drink, and relaxed his muscles for a few minutes. And each time he returned to the worksite, his muscles and his ax blade were renewed and ready to work more efficiently.

"I have a suggestion," Hiram said. "Tomorrow, if you like, we can alternate taking breaks at the top and bottom of each hour. Once an hour, you do what I did today: Go take a few minutes' break and get a drink of water while the ironsmith sharpens your blade. I'll continue to do the same. I'm confident that you'll keep up with me tomorrow."

His coworker agreed to try using Hiram's system for a day. Just as Hiram had predicted, the elder's production also increased dramatically. Of course, convinced of its wisdom and effectiveness, he continued using Hiram's system.

H iram's story has always been a visual reminder to me of the purely practical reasons to observe the Sabbath. Simply put, without this time of rest we burn out. For that reason I am careful to observe the Sabbath by ceasing my work one day out of the week.

This includes making certain that my servants and foreign laborers cease from their work on that seventh day.[8] During the construction of the Lord's Temple, a project that took seven years of work by many skilled craftsmen to complete, I was tempted a few times to allow our foreign workers—those who did not share the covenant heritage of the people of Israel and who did not observe the Sabbath—to continue working seven days a week.

But God revealed something to me that reminded me of the importance of following His laws in building the Temple. Here is what I heard:

> "As for this temple you are building, if you follow my decrees, carry out my regulations and keep all my commands and obey them, I will fulfill through you the promise I gave to David your father. And I will live among the Israelites and will not abandon my people Israel."[9]

I knew that this reminder from God concerning obedience to His laws included honoring the Sabbath. And I was reminded of two things. First of all, the Lord's law indicated that His people were to not only cease from working on the Sabbath, but also to make sure that those who worked for us ceased their work, even if they didn't share in our heritage or our faith.[10]

God's laws tell us that we should observe the Sabbath and that we should make sure that our servants do the same. Out of respect for God's wisdom—as well as for the memory of King Hiram's story—I give my laborers, even those who are not Israelites and therefore don't observe the Sabbath as a holy day, the seventh day off to rest and spend with their families.

Since I give my workers that day off, I have a rested and refreshed—and, therefore, a more effective—workforce. I believe that God has honored my decision to give my workers the Sabbath day off; I am convinced that a day of rest and renewal for every worker has assured us far superior productivity than if we worked seven days a week, week after week, to complete the project.

The superior output that has resulted from making certain my workers get this day of rest has shown me something: Obedience to the law of the Sabbath has great benefits for anyone who chooses that path, even those who don't have faith in the God of Israel, the God I serve.

That demonstrates well the truth I want you to learn. When you defeat the giant named Diversion, when you observe the principle of Sabbath rest, you will be blessed. Try it, and you just might find that your production will actually improve, even though the number of hours you work decreases. Not only that, you will also find your heart and mind renewed as you spend time away from your work.

Before we move on I want to take a few minutes to discuss the second reason for observing the Sabbath: To focus our attention on the God we are called to serve.

One of the songs my father did not write but that has been of much benefit to me says simply, "Be still, and know that I am God; I will be exalted among the nations, I will be exalted in the earth."[11]

When we walk in obedience, observing the principle of Sabbath rest, we defeat this giant named Diversion. When we do that, we give ourselves time to rest our minds and bodies. But even more importantly than that, we give ourselves a chance to be still before God, to acknowledge and thank Him for the good and perfect gifts He has poured out on us.

My father wrote a multitude of wonderful psalms, many of them during times when he rested before God and simply allowed himself to enjoy the Lord's presence. One of those psalms includes these words:

O God, you are my God, earnestly I seek you; my soul thirsts for you, my body longs for you, in a dry and weary land where there is no water. I have seen you in the sanctuary and beheld your power and your glory. Because your love is better than life, my lips will glorify you. I will praise you as long as I live, and in your name I will lift up my hands. My soul will be satisfied as with the richest of foods; with singing lips my mouth will praise you.[12]

These beautiful words came from a heart that took its time and focused on the Lord. My father realized well the value of taking time to be still before God, to focus on His wonderful attributes and on the great things He has done.

From the time I was a boy, my father taught me that I needed to have regular time when I could rest my body and my mind and focus on my Lord. I have found the Sabbath an ideal time to do just that.

I have learned that even in the busiest times in my life—and believe me, the building of the Temple was as busy a time as any I can remember—I need to honor the Sabbath by resting before and in my God.[13]

Hiram was right about refreshed workers who swing sharp axes—even the biggest trees in the forest are no match for them. Neither are the biggest giants. I'm glad, because they don't get any bigger than these next guys.

CHAPTER TEN

THE PROFANE
GIANT: DISRESPECT

My father used to tell me a story about an incident that took place during one particularly heavy military campaign the army of Israel was engaged in. One day, after an especially nasty skirmish, an officer brought before King David a young soldier who had, in the heat of battle, spoken disrespectfully the name of the God of Israel, an offense that was tantamount to treason among the soldiers in the army of the Lord.

My father told me that as he looked at that young man—trembling in fear because he knew how serious an offense it was among our people to abuse God's name—he was reminded of himself when he went up against the giant Goliath. This young man was roughly the same age and physical makeup David had been when he faced the Philistine.

Though my father recognized similarities between himself and this frightened young man, there was one profound difference: Even in his youth, my father understood the holiness of God's name. He drew confidence and strength from that marvelous name and for that reason was able to approach his first battlefield experience—against the best the Philistines had to offer—with a sense of destiny, a belief that God was with him and would bring him victory.

The young man who stood before my father didn't understand the importance of speaking the name of God only with honor and respect, of never misusing the name of the Lord. This young man, like so many other unsuspecting victims, had fallen prey to the vile giant named Disrespect.

The giant named Disrespect defeats us by minimizing our sense of awe and respect for the name of the Lord. When he is successful, he robs us of the blessings God wants to pour out upon those who properly revere His name, and he sets us up for the righteous judgment reserved for those who misuse the name of God.

My father had defeated Disrespect; he knew how vitally important it was that he treat God's name the way it deserved to be treated: honorably, respectfully, and with a deep sense of awe.

Friends, that is what enabled my father to defeat the mighty warrior Goliath all those years ago and what enabled him to lead so brilliantly as king of Israel for four decades. And it is what has allowed me to enjoy God's blessings in every area of my life.

The mere teenager stood in the name of our God against the awesome warrior named Goliath, and that gave him the ability to do what in human terms was impossible.

Allow me to read from the official record what transpired that day:

David said to the Philistine, "You come against me with sword and spear and javelin, but I come against you in the name of the LORD Almighty, the God of the armies of Israel, whom you have defied. This day the LORD will hand you over to me, and I'll strike you down and cut off your head. Today I will give the carcasses of the Philistine army to the birds of the air and the beasts of the earth, and the whole world will know that there is a God in Israel. All those gathered here will know that it is not by sword or spear that the LORD saves; for the battle is the LORD's, and he will give all of you into our hands."[1]

The official record indicates that Goliath, who had for forty days and forty nights bellowed threats and curses at the army of Israelites and at their God, didn't utter another word after the shepherd boy pronounced that he came in the name of the God of Israel and that the giant was going to die that day. Eyewitnesses who still live verify this as truth.

I now believe that had I been able to look over my father's shoulder into the eyes of the Philistine, I would have seen terror in the giant's eyes—the naked fear that would have come with the realization that he was about to enter into war with the very God of Israel.

King David told me many times that when he arrived in the valley that day and heard the brash and arrogant voice of a mere man defiling the name of his God, he remembered the words of Moses: "You shall not misuse the name of the LORD your God, for the LORD will not hold anyone guiltless who misuses his name."[2]

My father felt a sense of righteous anger at this man's insolence. He didn't care how tall Goliath was or what armaments he bore or what experience he had in battle, because he was confident that God had preordained him to win this battle.

Indeed, my father's pronouncement of death on Goliath came to pass. With one shot from his sling—he had packed five stones in his shepherd's bag that day, but only one would be needed—he dropped the awesome warrior in his tracks. The official record indicates that the stone actually sank into the giant's forehead, knocking him cold on the spot.[3]

In but a moment the giant's blasphemous tongue was silenced by a shepherd boy who came against him not with spears or javelins, but in the name of the Lord—that awesome, mighty, holy name.

Eyewitnesses later reported that the earth actually shook when Goliath fell. There's nothing about this in the official record, and I myself believe those reports are more than likely simple accounts of the moment's awesomeness. But there is one thing I know as fact: Something happened to the army of God when they saw the unconquerable giant topple.

Their hero slain, the Philistines turned in terror and ran. And the army that had to that point trembled at the sight of the giant went on to chase the Philistine army out of the land God had given them.[4]

What a day that must have been for the people of Israel!

Not only did they see a heroic victory by David and the Israelite army, they saw the very power of God at work on behalf of His people.

Faced with the threat of their very existence, the people of Israel were rescued by the man of God's own choosing, a man still in his teens, a man who didn't know how to use implements of war but who faced a mighty, awesome warrior bearing nothing but a sling and a pocketful of rocks.

Truly, those who were there that day witnessed firsthand the awesome power of the name of the Lord.

I n our culture, we hold the very name of our Lord and God in the highest esteem. We speak His name with a sense of awe and reverence, using adjectives such as *holy, awesome,* and *wonderful* to describe that name.

My father held the name of God in incredibly high regard and taught me much about how to speak the name of our Lord. He instructed me to exalt God's name,[5] take confidence in His name,[6] glorify His name,[7] praise His name,[8] and bless His name.[9]

My father never let me forget that in the law passed down through Moses, we as God's people have been warned to never misuse or disrespect God's name, that no one who speaks disrespectfully of His name will escape punishment.[10] He reminded me of the instructions we received to fear and honor God's awesome name,[11] that in the law there are specifically listed severe consequences for the misuse of God's name.[12]

My father taught me that the name of God as He revealed

Himself to us was His way of telling who He is and what He is really like. King David once said to me, "Son, I want to introduce you to *Jehovah Jireh*. He is the LORD who will provide."[13] Later he said, "Son, you need to pay your respect to *Jehovah Raffah*, the LORD who heals you."[14] On another occasion he told me, "Acquaint yourself with *Jehovah Nissi*, which means 'The LORD is my Banner.'"[15] Much later in his life, he said, "Solomon, your very name was given in honor of *Jehovah Shalom*, our LORD who is peace."[16]

My father's life was built around words he wrote prior to his death: "I will bless Thy name forever and ever."[17] He told me once, with tears in his eyes, that as God's people we are called to uphold and glorify the name of God in all we do and say. It is this way of living and thinking that made my father's life great, which led him to accomplish so many things on behalf of his God and his people.

And it's this way of living and thinking that he passed on to me.

God has allowed me to understand what my father knew so well: To treat God's holy, wonderful name with esteem and reverence is to treat God Himself in the same way. Conversely, uttering His name blasphemously is the same as treating God Himself disrespectfully.

Friends, if you want to be great in this life, you must give honor and glory to the name of the Lord. If you want to live a life of true and lasting peace and happiness, you need to make certain that your words honor and glorify the name of the Lord. If you want to be all God has created you to be, you will have to defeat this giant named Disrespect.

We live in a fallen world, a world filled with profanity. Irreverent talk—treating the sacred, holy name of God with contempt or disrespect—is rampant in every segment of our society.

Many a man perpetuates this type of speech almost proudly, voicing the word *God* in the context of cursing or swearing. He may not curse God directly, but he does it by carelessly and irreverently using His name. If you were to ask someone who practices this habit, he might tell you that he believes in and respects God—even if he doesn't know Him.

But I want us to think about something. If we are not careful, those of us who do know God can also be guilty of misusing His holy name. Think about it for a minute, and ask yourself if there aren't times when you have disrespectfully or irreverently used the name of God.

Do you ever use trite little phrases such as "Well, God forbid that I…" or "For the love of God!" or "Why, in God's name?" or "For God's sake!" as simple figures of speech, without the proper reverence for the name of God? Even using God's name as an exclamation is using His name disrespectfully, and it is a weapon of the giant named Disrespect, a weapon you need to remove from his possession.

Ask yourself if you have ever used God's name disrespectfully by speaking presumptuously. In other words, do you put words in God's mouth? Do you try to get what you want by speaking as if you somehow have an inside track on the will of God? Do you ever use phrases like "God told me…" or "It is God's will that…" in order to manipulate people into doing things you want them to do—things you may even *believe*

God wants them to do? When dealing with your family, do you ever threaten your children with warnings such as, "If you don't obey, God will get you"?

I believe that the reason my father was such a great defender of the Lord's name is because he started by examining his own heart for any disrespect or irreverence toward God. He taught me something valuable about searching my life for sin; I want to pass it on to you now. He wrote, "Search me, O God, and know my heart; test me and know my anxious thoughts. See if there is any offensive way in me, and lead me in the way everlasting."[18]

Search your heart and examine your life. If you have done any of those things, then you have used God's name in a manner that I refer to as spiritual forgery. I warn you to be very careful when you say what God's will is and isn't and what God will and will not be doing. God told the people of Israel to pay heed to His prophets, but the prophets themselves were told very specifically to be certain that the words they spoke were the words of God. For a prophet to speak otherwise was an offense that carried with it severe penalties.[19]

If you recognize any of these things in your own life, then you must purpose, with God's help, to make changes in how you treat the name of God. When you do that, you are one step closer to defeating the giant named Disrespect.

Clearly the way we use our Lord's name is of great importance to Him. God has said very specifically that those who use His name disrespectfully will not go unpunished. But at the same time, I know that our God is a God of forgiveness and restoration and that He is willing to bring those who misuse His name back into fellowship with Him—when we come to Him with hearts that are genuinely contrite.

The young soldier who stood before my father, charged with using our God's name disrespectfully, knew that he had done wrong. He was aware that, according to the law, he deserved to die. He fell before my father and begged for forgiveness and mercy for the sin he had committed against God.

My father extended mercy to the young man, but with a condition: "Young man," he said, "the Lord is our high commander and to speak against Him is to commit treason. But because of your youth, I am going to have mercy on you today. I never want to hear of you using such foolish talk again. When you speak the name of the Lord, remember whom you are speaking of, and make certain that what you say glorifies His name."

My father, seeing the sorrow in this young man's eyes when he fully realized what he had done, offered him forgiveness so far as he was able. Before he let the young man leave, however, he encouraged him to offer his repentance to the One who had ultimately been wronged.

"Young man, it was not my name but God's that you used in vain," the king said. "You'll need to seek His forgiveness. Go to Him; take your offerings and confess your sin. Then make sure that from now on your words never bring Him anything but the glory due Him as our Lord."

The young man did as King David had instructed him.

He left and immediately fell before God, begging for mercy and forgiveness. Not only did he never disrespectfully use God's name again, he also became a great defender and advocate of the name of the Lord.

He had defeated Disrespect. And God's blessing was on him.

If we make the stand this young man did, if we purpose in our hearts to defeat this enemy called Disrespect, God's favor will be on us as well. And trust me, we need all the favor we can get to escape the trap of this next giant. He's got more tricks than Pharaoh's magicians.

THE COUNTERFEIT GIANT: DUPLICITY

In Israel, our halls of justice are filled with dishonest merchants who might show an unsuspecting buyer an article of real gold, then defraud the customer. The merchant does that by performing a sleight of hand. After the seller accepts the money, he craftily replaces the authentic gold item with one made of what is called "fool's gold." The buyer slips the item into his bag believing that he has purchased a valuable item, an item of pure gold, only to find out later that what he really bought is nothing more than a cheap copy of the real thing.

At a glance, the counterfeit gold looks like the real thing. It has nearly the same color and texture as real gold. But when someone who knows what real gold looks like examines the item more closely, he sees that it is nearly worthless. In that case, the buyer has been duped by a counterfeit. He has traded something of real value—namely, his money—for something of little or no value.

If you think it foolish for a person to be deceived in this

way, I want you to take a moment to consider something. Far too many people—including people within my own kingdom—are taken in by counterfeits. They accept cheap knockoffs of a genuine article, an article of incredible worth. I'm not speaking of an item made from mere gold, but of an item worth far more than all the world's riches combined. I'm speaking of the God whom we are called to serve, the God who wants our undivided loyalty, the God who is Lord of everything.

You may ask what could possibly take the place of God Himself. You may wonder how we could trade in that which is eternal for that which is temporal. But there is something in each of us, within our fallen human nature, that makes it not just plausible for us to accept counterfeits, but remarkably easy.

I have known many people who place things such as self, career, money, and family above the One who is above all. I have seen those who in their quest for personal recognition and prestige displace the Lord from His rightful position in their hearts. If you were to ask these people what was number one in their lives, they would tell you that it's the true and living God, the *only* God. But their lives don't back up their words. They are people with divided hearts, people who are attempting to serve both God and this world.

Those whose hearts are divided in this way are at the mercy of the next giant I want to expose, the giant named Duplicity—or, as some might refer to him, the giant named the divided heart.

Duplicity is one of the craftiest giants any of us will ever face. He is underhanded in all his ways, and his mission is simple: He wants to divert our hearts and minds from the one true God. He wants us to be double-minded half-servants of a God who wants our total commitment and loyalty.

The giant named Duplicity wants us to believe in and serve *a* god. He wants us to talk to our friends, neighbors, and family members about our god. But he doesn't want us to serve the *one true* God. Oh, he doesn't mind if we believe in the God of Israel, the God my father served and the God I serve. This giant doesn't even mind if we serve Him in a half-hearted way. But the giant named Duplicity wants us to place our own personal god or gods before the one and only God who is worthy of preeminence in our hearts as Lord of all.

The giant named Duplicity uses our desires for wealth, power, recognition, and prestige to trap and defeat us. This is a crafty tactic because, as I pointed out earlier, there is nothing inherently wrong with the desire to achieve great things in this life. There is nothing evil about working hard for wealth or recognition. I myself have worked very hard and accomplished much in this world, both in my private life and as a servant of God and my nation. I know many great men who have also worked hard to achieve, and who have been able to keep their personal desires in check so as to serve God with all their hearts.

However, when we place our desires for material wealth, power, and recognition in the place reserved for the one who is above all, we fall into the trap Duplicity has set for us. And

I can tell you from the things I've witnessed that those desires can ensnare us much the same way hard drink, illicit affairs, or evil acts of any kind can.

When our desires for more money, more power, and more recognition control us, those things take the place of the one true God in our hearts. When we allow that to happen, we not only lose out on His blessings, we also risk having to suffer the consequences.

Many men and women on their journey to the promised land of true and lasting success have fought and conquered each of the giants we have discussed so far, only to be stopped cold by the giant named Duplicity.

This giant knows that most people will taste a certain degree of professional, financial, and social success at different points in their lives. But he also knows that there is something about our fallen human nature that makes us desire more and more. That desire for more leads us into lives of duplicity, which makes gods—idols, in other words—of things other than the Lord God Himself.

Unchecked desires for power, wealth, and prestige are nothing more than idolatry, forbidden by God in the law passed down through Moses:

> You shall have no other gods before me. You shall not make for yourself an idol in the form of anything in heaven above or on the earth beneath or in the waters below. You shall not bow down to them or worship

them; for I, the LORD your God, am a jealous God, punishing the children for the sin of the fathers to the third and fourth generation of those who hate me, but showing love to thousands who love me and keep my commandments.[1]

We need to take very seriously God's warning against placing anything above Him. But I believe there is more to it than that. You see, when we read of God passing down His prohibition against having gods *before* Him, we can read into that commandment that we are not to have any gods *other than* Him. That means, in other words, that there can be nothing else in our lives—not our money, our careers, our social standing, or our families—that holds a place comparable to that of our God.

Friends, God has made it very clear that not only will He not tolerate our forsaking Him for our own gods, He also won't share His position as our God with anyone or anything.

I've seen the folly of making the pursuit of earthly power into a god. I know that no matter what I achieve, no matter how much I possess, and no matter how highly esteemed I am, it will never be enough if I don't place those things at the feet of my Lord. If I allow the giant, Duplicity, to tempt me into making those things personal gods, I will never be satisfied.

To us who serve the one true God, earthly wealth in the form of money or possessions, status, power, and prestige are to mean nothing in comparison to the One we are to love with our whole beings—with our hearts, with our minds, with all of our strength.[2]

My father spoke often of how much he hated idolatry,[3] and he prayed continually for an undivided heart, a heart that worshiped only the true and living God.[4] He knew how vitally important it was for him to keep his focus on the Lord alone.

King David understood well the danger of placing his trust in earthly possessions, status, or reputation. He knew that he needed to place his trust in God and leave it there. He knew that his security and his rest were in God alone and that if he leaned on God in all his ways he would never be shaken.[5]

We should follow the example of King David, this man after God's own heart, in focusing our attention, adoration, and commitment on God who made us and who sustains us.

A s the king of Israel I can tell you that power, wealth, and prestige make excellent servants but pitiful gods. If we use them the way we should, these things can be useful tools. But when we don't keep them in their place, when we allow them to be the driving force for how we live our lives, they each cry out, "If you just possess more of me, I will make you happy! I will fulfill the longing in your soul. You'll have everything you've ever dreamed of."

Friends, you need to know that no matter what form a counterfeit god takes—be it money, status, or power—that god will most certainly let you down when you need it the most. That is because you have pledged your allegiance and your worship to that which is really no god at all.

Ask yourself these questions: Can earthly wealth (money, possessions, property) save you? Can your money prolong your life by one minute? Can your position in this world's system guarantee you a place in God's kingdom? Can everything you have in this world make you righteous in the eyes of God?

Clearly the answer to all those questions is a resounding "No!" What does it profit a man to gain the whole world and lose his very soul? Or what can a man give in exchange for his soul?[6]

Furthermore, I can tell you with great assurance that nothing satisfies the way our relationship with God can. The Creator has, by design, left a God-sized void in each of His creatures. Try as we might, nothing this world has to offer can fill that hole. So when we attempt to build our lives around anything but Him, we not only bring judgment upon ourselves, but we will always be left feeling unfulfilled and empty.

No matter how much you achieve, no matter how big your bank account is, no matter how much property you own, if your heart is divided from God, then it will never fulfill you. It will only leave you striving for more and—even if you get what you're chasing—enjoying it less. And it's that missing piece that results in a *missing peace*. By design, God says that there will be no lasting peace apart from the Prince of Peace.

The giant named Duplicity wants to send us on a never-ending cycle of attainment in which we constantly work to get more, only to find that getting more makes us desire *still more*. I have learned that an increase in power, wealth, or prestige will not rid me of the emptiness and dissatisfaction that come with being separated from God.[7]

The bottom line, friends, is that there is only one thing that will satisfy us in a deep, lasting way: It's knowing the God who with a word made all that we are and everything we do possible.

My father used to tell me that nothing—no earthly accomplishment or blessing, no level of monetary wealth, no elevated status in this world—could satisfy him more than the presence of God.[8] Nothing, he said, could be compared with the Lord.[9] My father conquered the giant named Duplicity simply because he wanted to be satisfied in God and God alone. That's one prayer that we can be certain He'll grant every time it's requested.

That is the way God designed each of us to live. You see, the Lord placed that God-shaped vacancy within the heart of each of us, and it can't be filled by any earthly god or idol. My father taught me that placing our trust in Him is our first key to bringing the giant named Duplicity to his knees, which is necessary if we are to live the kind of successful, blessed lives He intends for us to live.

God has created each of us to soar heavenward, but to do that we must learn to place Him on the throne of our lives, forsaking every counterfeit god Duplicity dangles before us. That is the all-important commitment we must make if we are to enjoy God's lasting blessing of true happiness and fulfillment in this life. And it's a pledge we must make if we are to be deemed worthy of serving Him in all we do.

I t may shock you to hear me say this, but if we are not willing to lay the things of this world at God's feet and abandon ourselves and all that we have to Him as an act of sacrificial love, then we are not worthy to serve Him at all. God wants hearts that are wholly committed to Him and to His ways.

Allow me to illustrate this point. If a wealthy merchant were to approach me and ask what he needed to do in order to enter into my service, I would do whatever I could to determine whether his allegiance would be to me or to the money, status, or access to power he would acquire. I might even tell him that he needed to rid himself of all he had by giving it away to the poor—just to see if he was more interested in serving his money or in serving me. If he was willing to do that, then I would gladly welcome him to my service; if not, I would likely reject him, because I would recognize him as a man with a divided heart.

As king of Israel, I have learned that it is not possible for a man to loyally serve two masters. This is also true of God: You can't simultaneously serve Him and money, power, or status. Sooner or later you will come to a point of resentment toward one of them.

I want you to think about something for a moment. If the Lord asked you to give up the most prized possession in your life—the thing that means more to you than anything else—in order to enter His kingdom, would you do it? *Could* you do it? Friends, this is the ultimate test, the superlative question you must apply to see if something has become an idol to you.

If you are unwilling to give away the earthly blessings you have received, if you are unable to lay aside the money, the prestige, and the power you have attained here and now, then you have come to a point where those things own you, and not the other way around. In that case, the giant named Duplicity has you cornered. You are foolishly attempting to serve two masters, and you will be thwarted in your attempts to reach the promised land of true and lasting success. Conversely, when you come to a point of being able to give away even your most valuable possessions, then you have taken a step toward conquering Duplicity.

Without a passionately single-minded approach to God, anything we can possess—even all the wealth and power and recognition the world has to offer—will mean nothing. And it is folly to place value on these things other than that which God intended.

What we have to ask ourselves is this: Do our possessions and status and power serve us, or do we serve them? Do we control these things, or do they control us? If we find ourselves serving our possessions or status, if we find that they have become a domineering factor in our lives, then they have become counterfeit gods to us.

If we find ourselves lured into the trap of becoming a servant to our riches, power, or status, then we must readjust our thinking, purify our hearts, and focus our attentions on the true, living God, the one who is the source of every blessing, both material and eternal.

On the other hand, you might naively believe that success doesn't have to be measured in the light of eternity—that if you've conquered giants ten through two then you have "arrived." Really? I thought your desired destination was the land known as *lasting success*. If that's true—and I hope it is— you've got one last giant looming large between you and your final reward. And, unfortuantely, your previous victories over those other giants won't help you one bit from this point on. The infamous Number One Giant is in a league all by himself.

CHAPTER TWELVE

THE UNAVOIDABLE GIANT: DEATH

To this point I have talked about nine extremely formidable and deadly giants who can, if we don't face up to them effectively, stop us on our journey toward the promised land of lasting success.

Early on I warned you that sooner or later you would face at least one of these personal giants. At any given point in your life you *may* face a giant named Discontent, Deception, Disregard, Division, or any of the others I've listed. Some of these giants you may not have to battle, but mark my words: You *will* have to battle at least one of them at some point in your earthly existence. He's the unavoidable giant named Death.

Let me introduce you to this giant by reading from the historical record of the nation of Israel.

Moses came with Joshua son of Nun and spoke all the words of this song in the hearing of the people. When Moses finished reciting all these words to all Israel, he said to them, "Take to heart all the words I have solemnly declared to you this day, so that you may command your children to obey carefully all the words of this law. They are not just idle words for you—they are your life. By them you will live long in the land you are crossing the Jordan to possess."

On that same day the LORD told Moses, "Go up into the Abarim Range to Mount Nebo in Moab, across from Jericho, and view Canaan, the land I am giving the Israelites as their own possession. There on the mountain that you have climbed you will die and be gathered to your people, just as your brother Aaron died on Mount Hor and was gathered to his people. This is because both of you broke faith with me in the presence of the Israelites at the waters of Meribah Kadesh in the Desert of Zin and because you did not uphold my holiness among the Israelites. Therefore, you will see the land only from a distance; you will not enter the land I am giving to the people of Israel."[1]

Later in the record, we see that Moses did indeed see from a distance the land of promise that God had deeded His chosen people, the Israelites. We also see that he died soon after, just as God had told him he would:

Then Moses climbed Mount Nebo from the plains of Moab to the top of Pisgah, across from Jericho. There the LORD showed him the whole land—from Gilead to Dan, all of Naphtali, the territory of Ephraim and

Manasseh, all the land of Judah as far as the western sea, the Negev and the whole region from the Valley of Jericho, the City of Palms, as far as Zoar. Then the LORD said to him, "This is the land I promised on oath to Abraham, Isaac and Jacob when I said, 'I will give it to your descendants.' I have let you see it with your eyes, but you will not cross over into it."

And Moses the servant of the LORD died there in Moab, as the LORD had said. He buried him in Moab, in the valley opposite Beth Peor, but to this day no one knows where the grave is. Moses was a hundred and twenty years old when he died, yet his eyes were not weak nor his strength gone. The Israelites grieved for Moses in the plains of Moab thirty days, until the time of weeping and mourning was over.[2]

Tragically, Moses—the man God chose to lead the people of Israel out of their captivity to the Egyptians, the man God used to bring His chosen people His holy law, the man who interceded before God on behalf of his people—was stopped short of actually entering into the Promised Land. The great prophet and mighty servant of God tasted death before he tasted of God's ultimate blessing for His people.[3]

That is how the giant named Death works. He seeks to block all of us from entering the promised land of ultimate success. He seeks with all his might to overtake us before we can become all that God intends for us to be. He's a giant whose goal is to take everything from us, starting with our very existence. And, tragically, he is a giant who has an appointment with each and every one of us.

I f there is an ultimate destiny in life, it is a one-time
appointment with this giant, Death.[4] Ultimately, none
of us will escape death. In the words of our prophets,
"What man can live and not see death, or save himself from
the power of the grave?"[5]

The death rate is presently hovering at 100 percent. Each
of us is going to die.

We can do the things it takes to keep our bodies healthy,
we can live clean lives, and we can obey every one of God's
moral laws, yet we will still eventually die. At a time
appointed by God, each of us will face the end of our physical existence. When that occurs, our opportunities for serving God, our families, and our friends here on earth will
cease forever. When we die, we have no more chances to
achieve great things in this world.

It is true that each of us must face death, a fact made all
the more tragic if you consider that perhaps it doesn't have
to end that way. Suppose He intended that we live in a perfect place in perfect harmony with Him, our fellow humans,
and all of creation—what if God never meant for physical
death to be the final part of the equation? What if nothing
were able to come between us and God? What if there were
no giants to terrorize us, including this giant named Death?

But this beautiful picture of eternal harmony was ruined
when the first two people on record chose the path of disobedience to God. With that, sin—rebellion against the
Creator—entered the picture, and the giant named Death
rudely made his first appearance to mankind.

Originally, God's creation was perfect, and that included

its inhabitants. Adam and Eve, the crowning jewels of God's perfect creation, had their run of Paradise. Their only purposes in life were to care for the Garden of Eden and to enjoy close, intimate fellowship with God and with each other. They had perfect harmony with creation around them and with God who created it. They could go anywhere in the Garden and do anything they wanted.

God told Adam and Eve that they could eat anything in that beautiful Garden, with one exception: "You are free to eat from any tree in the garden, but you must not eat from the tree of the knowledge of good and evil, for when you eat of it you will surely die."[6]

Certainly the prohibition was easy to understand. "Don't eat from this tree!" God said. The consequence for disobedience was clear: *You will surely die!* It wasn't a complicated equation. It was simply "Eat, and you die." We know that the first couple didn't want to die. But our ultimate enemy, the evil force that opposes all that is holy, lured the first humans into spiritual treason against their Creator.

The official record as Moses himself recorded it tells us that the serpent gave the giant named Death the "in" he needed when he planted doubt in the minds of the man and woman concerning God's warning against eating the fruit: "Did God really say, 'You must not eat from any tree in the garden'?" the serpent asked. "You will not surely die. For God knows that when you eat of it your eyes will be opened, and you will be like God, knowing good and evil."[7]

If sin weren't initially sweet—long before the bitter sting—then none of us would choose it. Likewise the serpent's proffer was very convincing, and the fruit certainly did look tempting. And so the woman did what she had been told specifically not to do: She ate of it, then offered some to her husband. He, too, chose to partake. Immediately, these two people knew they had done wrong, so they hid themselves—from one another and from God. Before long, however, the Lord called them out for what they had done.[8]

The result of this disobedience was what we now call "the curse." Everything around us was cursed: our relationships, our work, even the very ground we walk on. Worst of all, however, was God's pronouncement of death on every member of the human race. "For dust you are and to dust you will return," He told them.[9]

With that, the giant named Death had gained a foothold over all of humanity. Because of the original sin committed by Adam and Eve, you will die. You may think it's unfair—but it is true. Whether you are rich or poor, powerful or weak, big or small, you will inevitably meet this giant, Death.

When my father squared off against Goliath the Philistine, the stakes were high indeed. David was in a fight for his life with a man who, by all accounts, had no fear of losing to this mere shepherd boy. But the stakes were much higher than my father's destiny as winner of this battle; had Goliath won, the people of Israel would have been taken captive by the Philistines.

By now you know that my father won a mighty and miraculous victory over the giant and that the Israelite army went on to rout the Philistines. Through that victory, God preserved Israel's place as His own chosen race. And David, whose name became a symbol of courage, obedience, and heroism among our people and among the other peoples of the earth, went on to serve gloriously and triumphantly as king of Israel.

Despite all that, he, like everyone who had gone before him, had an appointment with the giant named Death. My father kept his appointment and the giant won.

Not long ago I visited the gravesite of my father, the once-great warrior and king of our nation. As I looked at his grave, I thought of all the great things King David had done for his people in the service of his God. I thought about the kingdom God had used him to establish, the victories he had won, the leadership he had provided, and the wisdom he had passed on to those around him.

Then I thought about the bottom-line truth King David's grave presented to me: No matter what we accomplish in this life, no matter how educated, wealthy, or powerful we are on life's journey, we will eventually lose our personal battle with this giant named Death.

It reminded me that I am destined to die—despite my earthly wealth, despite the things God has allowed me to accomplish in the kingdom, despite the wisdom with which He has blessed me, and despite my own successes and failures.

My father, who by all accounts was the greatest king Israel ever knew, faced down that giant named Death. And so will I.

So will you.

The law, the moral and spiritual code of conduct God passed on to His people through Moses, gives us weapons to battle the nine giants we've discussed so far. With their eyes on this law, many in Moses' generation—and in subsequent generations—defeated the giant named Discontent and laid aside their covetous ways. Others have defeated the giants named Deception, Division, Disrespect, and Duplicity.

God's holy commandments give us the motivation to defeat these first nine giants. Indeed, these commandments are powerful weapons we can use against these giants. But when we go into battle against the final giant, Death, the law is powerless. In other words, we may gain victory over our own dishonesty, but we will still die eventually. We may lay aside all greed and covetousness, but there will come a time when our physical existence ends. We may be completely faithful to our spouses and our God, but we will eventually pass from this existence into eternity.

You may listen to what I'm saying here and ask, "Does this mean that the relentless giant named Death accomplished what Goliath could not? Does this mean there can be no victory over this destroyer?"

I want you to know that the answer to both of those questions is a resounding "No!" Although we are all appointed a time to die physically, there is hope for ultimate victory over Death. I'm not suggesting that there is a way to avoid our appointment with physical death, only that we needn't be eternally defeated by this giant.

Where do I find that hope, you ask? I want to tell you that you can find hope in the clues God has given us.

Throughout the history of our people, God has used men and women of His own choosing to deliver messages we needed to hear. That is His divine plan. The Lord used Moses to deliver the people of Israel from slavery to the Egyptians,[10] and He used my father to deliver us from the threat of the giant Goliath.[11] Likewise, He will use another deliverer to free His people from the ultimate power of the giant we call Death.[12]

In God's covenant with my father at the time he was crowned king of Israel, it was established that an offspring of David would be the one to deliver our nation and every other nation from the giant named Death.[13]

Although I am an offspring of David, I can tell you with certainty something about this promised deliverer: I'm not Him! So if you are looking to enter the promised land of lasting success, it will not happen by placing your trust in me but rather by placing your trust in Him who shall be known as the One Greater than Solomon,[14] the Messiah whose mission was established before the world was created: to conquer with finality this giant named Death by destroying the works of the evil one.[15]

From the very beginning, my people have been waiting and watching for the arrival of God's Chosen One, our Messiah,[16] the Anointed One of God, who alone has the ultimate power over the giant named Death. It is the same Deliverer of whom God foretold, through my father, all those years ago.[17]

In the record of what happened back in the Garden of Eden—where the giant named Death made his first appearance to humankind—we can read about God's judgment on the serpent when He announced that the Savior of the world would be the offspring of a woman.[18]

Later on, we read of God's promise to father Abraham that all the people of the world would be blessed through his offspring because of his obedience.[19] Our own prophecies also indicate that this God-man will descend from our own tribe of Judah,[20] and that He will endure injustices on our behalf, including being lied about,[21] being mocked and insulted,[22] being hated without cause,[23] being betrayed by a close friend for thirty pieces of silver,[24] and being pierced in His hands and feet.[25]

In spite of all this, *Yeshua HaMashiach*—in my Hebrew language, the Chosen One—the Son of God we are eagerly awaiting, will conquer death by rising from the grave[26] and ascending to heaven,[27] where He will rejoin our Father God and mediate with Him on our behalf.[28]

My father, in his battle with Goliath, listened as the giant bellowed threats he couldn't back up. He later said that the only way the giant could have defeated him was if he had allowed it. Goliath promised that there would be death on the battlefield that day, then charged at my father with his spear, sword, and javelin. But because my father's faith was in the God of the Living who sent him into battle, he defeated the giant named Goliath at the Valley of Elah and he most certainly will conquer the giant named Death in the presence of the Resurrection.[29]

Each of us is destined for an appointment with physical

death.[30] Each of us will cross over from this life into the next. And because there will come unto us a prophet like unto Moses[31] who will defeat for all eternity the giant named Death, we can know that even though our outward man wastes away, our inward man is being renewed day by day through faith in Him whose kingdom shall never end.[32]

And one day as God's people from every tribe and nation, from every generation, kneel in the presence of the King of kings, we will hear those glorious words, "Well done, My good and faithful servant, enter into the joy that I have prepared for you."[33]

I can picture our High Commander saying, "You have battled and beaten those giants named Discontent, Deception, and Disregard, and what you experienced by faith during your earthly journey shall be your estate forever. I shall supply all your needs according to My riches in glory![34]

"You have dared and defeated the giants named Division, Destruction, and Dishonor, and what you saw through a glass dimly is now revealed with perfect clarity: Behold what manner of love I have bestowed upon you, that you should be called the children of God![35]

"You have challenged and conquered Diversion, Disrespect, and Duplicity, and you are living witnesses that whosoever is born of God overcomes the world. And today, in the land of the living, you can see that your confidence was not in vain: I began a good work in you, and I have been faithful to complete it.[36]

"Yes, I am the Resurrection[37] and the Life and even that last giant, Death, has been swallowed up in victory.[38] No weapon that was formed against you has prospered; and every tongue that rose against you has been condemned.[39] This was, and is, and forever shall be the heritage of My people. Enter into the land I promised you, for you are truly more than conquerors!"[40]

The publisher and author would love to hear your comments about this book. *Please contact us at:* www.multnomah.net/giants

ENDNOTES

CHAPTER ONE

1. 1 Samuel 17:33
2. 1 Samuel 17:34–37

CHAPTER TWO

1. 1 Samuel 17:48
2. 1 Samuel 17:8–9
3. 1 Samuel 17:8–10
4. Proverbs 29:18
5. Numbers 13:1–14:30
6. 1 Samuel 17:32
7. 1 Samuel 16:12–13
8. Luke 16:10

CHAPTER THREE

1. Ecclesiastes 5:10
2. Romans 8:28
3. Ecclesiastes 5:12
4. Proverbs 3:13–18
5. Deuteronomy 8:18
6. Ecclesiastes 5:15

CHAPTER FOUR

1. Proverbs 18:21
2. Exodus 20:16
3. Exodus 23:1
4. Romans 6:23

5. Proverbs 10:9
6. Proverbs 19:1

Chapter Five

1. Psalm 112:5
2. Proverbs 11:25
3. Proverbs 22:9
4. Ecclesiastes 5:10
5. Genesis 22:9–13
6. Job 1:21

Chapter Six

1. 2 Samuel 11
2. Acts 13:22
3. 2 Samuel 12:5–6
4. 2 Samuel 12:13
5. Psalm 103:3–4
6. Ecclesiastes 5:4
7. Exodus 20:14
8. 1 Samuel 12:24
9. Proverbs 28:20
10. Psalm 18:25
11. Proverbs 2:8

Chapter Seven

1. 1 Samuel 17:10
2. 1 Samuel 17:32–37
3. 1 Samuel 17:43–44
4. Genesis 4
5. Genesis 37

6. 1 Samuel 17:45–46
7. 1 Samuel 18:7
8. 1 Samuel 18–19
9. Exodus 20:13
10. Deuteronomy 7:12
11. Psalm 57:3
12. Leviticus 19:18
13. Proverbs 16:24; 21:23
14. Proverbs 15:1
15. Matthew 12:34
16. Proverbs 14:9
17. 2 Samuel 11–12
18. Psalm 15:2
19. Luke 18:27

CHAPTER EIGHT

1. 1 Kings 2:1–3
2. 1 Kings 2:10–12
3. Exodus 20:12
4. Exodus 20:12
5. Deuteronomy 4:9; 6:5–7
6. Exodus 21:15, 17
7. Proverbs 23:22
8. Proverbs 22:6

CHAPTER NINE

1. Proverbs 10:4
2. Exodus 20:8–11
3. Psalm 46:10
4. Genesis 2:2–3

5. Leviticus 25:1–7
6. 2 Samuel 5:11–12
7. I Kings 5–6
8. Exodus 20:10
9. 1 Kings 6:12–13
10. Exodus 20:10
11. Psalm 46:10
12. Psalm 63:1–5
13. Psalm 62:1

CHAPTER TEN

1. 1 Samuel 17:45–47
2. Exodus 20:7
3. 1 Samuel 17:48–49
4. 1 Samuel 17:51–53
5. Psalm 34:3
6. Psalm 20:7
7. Psalm 66:2
8. Psalm 68:4
9. Psalm 145:1
10. Exodus 20:7
11. Deuteronomy 28:58
12. Leviticus 24:10–16
13. Genesis 22:14
14. Exodus 15:26
15. Exodus 17:15
16. Judges 6:24
17. Psalm 145:1
18. Psalm 139:23–24
19. Deuteronomy 18:14–22

ENDNOTES

CHAPTER ELEVEN

1. Exodus 20:3–6
2. Deuteronomy 6:5
3. Psalm 31:6
4. Psalm 86:11
5. Psalm 62:1–2
6. Matthew 16:26
7. Ecclesiastes 5:10–18
8. Psalm 86:8
9. Psalm 89:6

CHAPTER TWELVE

1. Deuteronomy 32:44–52
2. Deuteronomy 34:1–8
3. Deuteronomy 32:52
4. Ecclesiastes 7:2
5. Psalm 89:48
6. Genesis 2:16–17
7. Genesis 2:16–17
8. Genesis 3:6–8
9. Genesis 3:14–19
10. Exodus 3:7–10
11. 1 Samuel 17:45–47
12. Psalm 49:15
13. 2 Samuel 7:17
14. Matthew 12:42
15. John 3:1
16. Psalm 110:1–2
17. Psalm 29:1–11

18. Genesis 3:15
19. Genesis 18:18; 22:18; 26:4–5
20. Genesis 49:10
21. Psalm 27:12
22. Psalm 22:6–8
23. Psalm 69:4
24. Psalm 41:9
25. Psalm 22:16
26. Psalm 16:10
27. Psalm 68:18
28. 1 Timothy 2:5
29. Isaiah 25:8
30. Hebrews 9:27–28
31. Deuteronomy 18:15
32. Luke 1:33
33. Matthew 25:21
34. Philippians 4:15
35. 1 John 3:1
36. Philippians 1:6
37 John 11:23–26
38. 1 Corinthians 15:54–55
39. Isaiah 54:17
40. Romans 8:37